The Winning Message

Candidate Behavior, Campaign Discourse, and Democracy

This study breaks new ground in investigating candidate behavior in American electoral campaigns. It centers on a question of equal importance to citizens and scholars: How can we produce better political campaigns? The project takes an innovative approach to answering this question by bringing together critical and empirical methods as well as game theory in a sophisticated yet readable text. The answer comes in four parts. First, Simon develops the idea of dialogue as a standard for evaluating political campaigns. Second, he shows that candidates' self-interest in winning leads them to avoid dialogue, which is substantive campaign discourse. Third, he demonstrates the beneficial effects produced by the little dialogue that actually occurs. Fourth, he pinpoints the forces responsible for these rare occurrences. The major lesson of this work is that campaign reform under its present guise will not bring about the more substantive campaigns that the public desires.

ADAM F. SIMON is assistant professor of political science, University of Washington. He received his Political Science Ph.D. in 1997 from the University of California, Los Angeles. He was a National Science Foundation Graduate Fellow. His work has appeared in the *American Political Science Review* and the *Journal of Communication*, as well as other scholarly journals.

D0967913

Politics and relations among individuals in societies across the world are being transformed by new technologies for targeting individuals and sophisticated methods for shaping personalized messages. The new technologies challenge boundaries of many kinds – between news, information, entertainment, and advertising; between media, with the arrival of the World Wide Web; and even between nations. *Communication, Society and Politics* probes the political and social impacts of these new communication systems in national, comparative, and global perspective.

The Winning Message

CANDIDATE BEHAVIOR, CAMPAIGN
DISCOURSE, AND DEMOCRACY

Adam F. Simon
University of Washington

CAMBRIDGE
UNIVERSITY PRESS

PUBLISHED BY THE PRESS SYNDICATE OF THE UNIVERSITY OF CAMBRIDGE
The Pitt Building, Trumpington Street, Cambridge, United Kingdom

CAMBRIDGE UNIVERSITY PRESS
The Edinburgh Building, Cambridge CB2 2RU, UK
40 West 20th Street, New York, NY 10011-4211, USA
477 Williamstown Road, Port Melbourne, VIC 3207, Australia
Ruiz de Alarcón 13, 28014 Madrid, Spain
Dock House, The Waterfront, Cape Town 8001, South Africa

http://www.cambridge.org

© Adam F. Simon 2002

First published 2002

Printed in the United Kingdom at the University Press, Cambridge

Typefaces Minion 11/13 pt. and Centaur   *System* QuarkXPress [BTS]

A catalog record for this book is available from the British Library.

Library of Congress Cataloging in Publication Data
Simon, Adam F., 1965–
The winning message : candidate behavior, campaign discourse, and democracy /
Adam F. Simon.
p.   cm. – (Communication, society, and politics)
Includes bibliographical references and index.
ISBN 0-521-80733-6 – ISBN 0-521-00191-9 (pb.)
1. Politics, Practical – United States.   2. Political participation – United States.
3. Political campaigns – United States.   4. United States – Politics and government.
I. Title.   II. Series.
JK1726 .S55 2002
324.7'0973–dc21   2001035670

ISBN 0 521 80733 6 hardback
ISBN 0 521 00191 9 paperback

This book is dedicated to my parents –
Shirley and David Simon

Contents

Figures

Tables

Acknowledgments

Many people have participated in this project in one way or another. If this listing is incomplete or does not do full justice to an individual's contribution, I apologize. To start with, I would like to express my gratitude to all the people who helped with the data collection. Starting with the experiments conducted in 1994 at UCLA, I greatly appreciate the efforts of Leila Moyari, Bonnie Lemon, and David Willis, which were directed toward running the subjects (to whom I also owe a debt) and organizing the data. Also with respect to the experiments, I would like to recognize the generosity of the National Science Foundation, Shanto Iyengar, and The John and Mary Merkle Foundation for their support.

The content analyses were conducted at UCLA as well as the University of Washington, and I would like to thank all the undergraduates at both institutions who performed the coding. I also owe a debt of gratitude to Vincent Hutchings who helped design and execute the coding scheme, and Tracy Sulkin, who provided invaluable research assistance during the completion of the coding project. Lance Bennett, the Shorenstein Center at the John F. Kennedy School of Government, and the University of Washington's Royalty Research Fund all supplied financial assistance to support the coding effort. I owe a special thank you to Mark Hunt, who took the lead in creating the data on Senate candidate positions.

Many friends, teachers, and colleagues provided insight and ideas during the data analyses and preparation of this manuscript. At UCLA, the site of my graduate education, I would like to acknowledge Susanne Lohmann, Stephen Ansolabehere, Brian Walker, Diane Klein, John Petrocik, Shelley Taylor, John Zaller, and, especially, Shanto Iyengar, my dissertation advisor and mentor. At the University of Washington, my current institution, I gratefully recognize Tracy Sulkin, John Wilkerson,

Margaret Levi, Lance Bennett, and Bryan Jones. I would also like to thank panel participants at the annual meetings of the Midwest and American Political Science Associations.

Finally, I would like to thank Cambridge University Press, especially Lewis Bateman, the political science editor, Michael Moscati, his assistant, Lia Pelosi, the copy editor, and Pam Benjamin.

CHAPTER 1

Introduction

Observers of American elections regularly bemoan the lack of substance in contemporary political campaigns. However, while the need for substance has been clearly articulated, the remedy is not so apparent. Meanwhile, a sea change in the conduct of American politics continues to increase the public's dependence on campaigns for political information. The traditional competition between parties has evolved into a clash of candidates. This clash increasingly occurs over the airwaves and through other means of direct contact, largely at the expense of previous mechanisms that mediated contact between politicians and the public. For voters, the campaign is the proximate source of information about the candidates and the most immediate influence on their decision. For candidates, the campaign offers the best opportunity to hear the public's voice, to clarify long-term goals, and to establish immediate political priorities. Thus, the lack of substance alarms citizens and scholars alike and underscores the importance of an investigation of the dynamics supporting substantive campaigns. In what follows, I attempt to expose the roots of this problem and then to isolate the factors that either elevate or debase campaign discourse.

My examination is built around a minimal standard for normatively acceptable campaigns, called dialogue. Simply put, dialogue means that when one candidate raises a subject, his or her opponent responds by discussing the same subject. The opposite of dialogue is ignoring, responding by discussing a different subject. I rely on the work of leading political theorists and social critics to build a case for using dialogue as the criterion to evaluate contemporary campaigns, arguing that the standards for public discourse they propose entail a minimal requirement for dialogue. The concept of dialogue then bridges the normative discussion of campaigns and actual practice. My research into the dynamics supporting dialogue follows a social scientific approach, using several methodologies – game theory, experimental designs, content analysis, and sample surveys. Each method offers a unique strength in terms of investigating the phenomenon of campaign discourse, and, in combination, they create a robust understanding of the process and consequence of campaign communication.

Many features recommend dialogue as a yardstick for evaluating the quality of a campaign. In general, it is difficult to define and measure campaign substance, so a study of this kind must first establish a reasonably acceptable standard for campaign discourse that is also empirically useful. Simple assessments as to whether a particular campaign message is substantive are likely to be unsatisfactory. In the first place, almost every act or utterance can be construed as having some substantive content. The literature offers examples ranging from erudite policy analysis to the mundane act of eating a tamale incorrectly (Popkin 1991). More importantly, a simple way of measuring substance would neither account for the campaign's interactive nature nor allow us to engage in overall comparisons across campaigns. With the approach I take, it is clear that a partially substantive campaign is not one in which some messages are judged substantive and others are judged "fluff." Rather, a partially substantive campaign is characterized by constructive engagement for an observable proportion of the campaign's duration.

In constructing this yardstick for campaigns, I rely heavily on the work of democratic and critical theorists. What does (or more properly should) our society want in a campaign? Paraphrasing Kelley (1960), Bennett (1992), and others, the preelection campaign should educate voters to enable them to make an informed decision, and thereby clearly communicate their preferences to elected officials. As has been argued by nearly all democratic theorists, the best means to this end is free and open public discussion. Simplifying these complex normative theories, I argue that John Stuart Mill's notion of the marketplace of ideas and Jurgen Habermas's ideal speech situation both presume a minimal normative requirement for public speech that can be applied to campaign discourse. The unspoken premise running through these essays is the necessity for dialogue. Because of its position as a necessary condition for rational discourse, the level of dialogue approximates the quality of the campaign, where more is better.

Dialogue requires the cooperation or at least the acquiescence of both candidates. To state the obvious, an individual candidate cannot dialogue. Dialogue occurs only when two candidates address the same subject. The decision to dialogue can be construed as a strategic choice, so this construct can be used to dissect the behavior of candidates who pursue rational strategies in the hope of winning elections. Faced with an opponent's initiative, a candidate can choose to ignore it and raise a different subject, or a candidate can choose to respond on that subject. A response creates dialogue and opens the door to debate – an absence of dialogue blocks the direct route to meaningful communication. Game theory provides a tool to model these interactions, which are responsible for creating campaign discourse.

My game-theoretic model, some of whose assumptions are verified with an experimental design, condenses a large portion of the relevant research on voting behavior and campaign communication in the service of explaining the conditions that lead to dialogue. Given the assumption that candidates behave rationally when constructing campaign messages, the model yields a deductive proscription against dialogue. This preliminary result is confirmed using experimental and survey data from the 1994 California gubernatorial race. In this election, a candidate self-consciously dedicated to dialogue ran against a candidate equally self-consciously dedicated to pursuing victory by other means. The defeat of the candidate who attempted to dialogue (Democrat Kathleen Brown) provides a cautionary tale for those who believe in the potential for dialogue in any strong form in contemporary campaigns.

Dialogue is readily observable in everyday politics, as evidenced by some common expressions that signify the absence of dialogue – changing the subject, or "ducking an issue," for instance. Dialogue of some kind appears in almost every election, and these instances identify which levers to use to enhance political discourse. I refine my model and develop testable hypotheses to explain these appearances. First, some dialogue can be explained as the result of the media's editorial policies. Second, dialogue emerges from the "irrational" actions of certain candidates; for example, those who make mistakes or violate the model's assumptions. Third, some dialogue can be focused, intense, and substantive, when the campaign's psychological arena (public opinion) is effectively limited to one dimension, as in so-called critical elections (Burnham 1970). Using an exhaustive content analysis of almost fifty U.S. Senate elections, supported by background and survey data, I test for the appearance of dialogue under these circumstances.

This project, then, can be seen as an attempt to illustrate and investigate the tension between candidates' self-interest in winning and the collective interest in furthering democratic ideals. To articulate the polity's collective interest in campaigns as information-supplying institutions I develop the metaphor of a campaign as a political conversation as opposed to a political game. The decisive feature of this metaphor is the importance of dialogue in public discourse. The formal model takes up the game metaphor, which dominates current thinking about campaigns, and explains the absence of dialogue. Refinements of the model also pinpoint some special circumstances that support dialogue and higher quality discourse. Two sets of empirical analysis support these arguments: The first focuses on the causes of the absence of dialogue and is based on experimental data; the second focuses on special circumstances promoting dialogue and is based on a correlational analysis. Thus, the concept of dialogue captures the normative claims made by leading thinkers, addresses the interactive nature of the campaign and is capable of serving as a focus of empirical examination.

OUTLINE OF SUBSEQUENT CHAPTERS

In chapter two, I provide a justification for using dialogue as a normative standard for campaign discourse. First, I recount the observations of political spectators over the past hundred years who have highlighted the tendency for candidates to "talk past each other." Starting with the claim that campaigns are worthy of critical examination, I move on to discuss how an ideal campaign discourse would appear, taking my cue from the existing literature on public discourse, especially Habermas's notion of an ideal speech situation. In so doing, I also try to point out the special features of campaigns. Further, in order to underscore the significance of this study, I rehearse arguments that link the quality of public discourse to the legitimacy of democratic governance. With the normative view clarified, I propose dialogue as a standard consistent with that vision. I conclude by contrasting the game and conversational metaphors for campaigns.

In chapter three, I trace the relevant empirical literature that bears on understanding the origins and nature of campaign discourse. I begin with the contributions of three schools of political science research, the Michigan approach to the study of voting, the Rochester approach to the analysis of the behavior of rational candidates, and the "low-information rationality" perspective on voting in mass elections. I then synthesize these literatures into a nascent theory of campaigns in mass elections. This theory identifies the forces that impel or dissuade candidates from adopting campaign communication strategies that produce dialogue. I then briefly discuss the social scientific methodologies that are employed in subsequent analyses and outline my research design.

In chapter four, I develop a formal model that highlights the pressures on candidates to avoid discussing minority-held views and, thus, to avoid dialogue. I assume candidates are rational and model their behavior around a representation of voting and a typology of potential campaign effects. I claim every voter sums a number of different considerations, weighted in proportion to their importance. The typology consists of three well-researched effects: priming, learning, and direct persuasion. Taken as a whole, this typology describes the net effect of campaign communication on vote choice. Within this framework, candidates choose to discuss the set of themes that they expect will maximize their share of the electoral vote. The fundamental result is that engaging in dialogue is a dominated strategy. The open debate regarded as a mainstay of democratic decision making will never occur if candidates behave as the model dictates.

My approach diverges from other formal models of elections in important respects. Voters are taken to behave sincerely, an assumption that formalizes the well-researched psychological process underlying vote choice. The model is multidimensional. Finally, consistent with empirical research, I assume candidates have exogenous positions that are fixed for the duration of the campaign. These modifications, taken together, lead to a better fit between the model and the actual practice of campaigns.

In chapter five, I verify the ineffectiveness of dialogue as a vote-getting strategy with a case study of the 1994 California gubernatorial election. I chose this race because it pitted an incumbent, Pete Wilson, known for his use of contemporary campaign techniques, against a challenger, Kathleen Brown, who explicitly adhered to a strategy of dialogue. An experimental design employing actual ads shown to adult voters was administered during the campaign, which shows that the strategy of ignoring an opponent's message generates a better return than engaging in dialogue. When subjects saw Kathleen Brown discussing crime and immigration, the very themes Wilson advanced, she lost ground; when she discussed the economy and education, she gained. Likewise, when subjects saw Wilson discussing Brown's themes, he lost, but in conditions where he stayed "on message," he won. I analyze the experimental dataset further insofar as it allows the assessment of some of the modeling assumptions. To provide better grounds from which to generalize these results, the success of Wilson's strategy and the failure of Brown's is confirmed using poll data taken from the California poll.

In chapter six, I take the study of dialogue from the laboratory into the real world of campaigns with a study of dialogue in U.S. Senate elections. One major paper in each of forty-nine states is sampled from the elections of 1988, 1990, and 1992. The text of all the articles mentioning either candidate in the race were downloaded and coded according to the scheme devised to capture the amount of discussion generated by each candidate on thirty-two dimensions. In all over 6,700 articles were coded – almost a half a million lines of text. Using this data, three continuous measures of dialogue were constructed – instant dialogue, which measures dialogue appearing within the same article, sustained dialogue, which taps the amount of discussion of minority-held views over the course of a campaign, and a composite indicator, which combines the previous two. As expected the study reveals that the amount of dialogue, by any measure, present in these campaigns was quite low. I then digress to analyze the effects of dialogue on various measures of voter information and vote quality. This analysis documents that the presence of dialogue leads to a more informed and "better" electorate.

In chapter seven, I outline the prerequisites for meaningful dialogue in terms of the candidates' incentive structure and other background factors. Dialogue of a kind appears, albeit rarely, in almost every electoral campaign, casting doubts on my absolute proscription. By refining the model further, I attempt to explain the presence of these few instances of dialogue and to isolate those factors responsible for its appearance. The editorial policy of a paper or the political culture of a given region can drive the appearance of dialogue. Mistakes or violations of assumptions also play a clear role in the appearance of dialogue. For example, some candidates have no realistic chance of winning, so a rational model cannot explain their campaign behavior. This kind of dialogue is outside the model's purview. On the other hand, special cases produce explainable and meaningful dialogue. When the campaigners are effectively limited to discussing one issue or a cluster of closely correlated issues, as in so-called critical elections, a dialogue will occur.

In chapter eight, I summarize and draw conclusions. I discuss a weaker kind of dialogue called reframing. This distinction is subtle and involves cases where a psuedodialogue does not threaten a candidate's electoral prospects. I discuss some of the attempts to reframe dimensions in recent presidential contests, identifying them as fruitful areas for future research. I then review the lessons of this project, including an essay as to what campaign reform can and cannot accomplish.

CHAPTER 2

Dialogue: A Standard for Campaign Discourse

In this chapter, I present an argument for the use of dialogue as a normative standard to evaluate the quality of political campaigns. The argument relies on an ideal for candidate behavior derived from claims advanced by theorists, especially Habermas, in examinations of public discourse. (To preview, chapters three and four outline a theory of candidate message selection that describes actual candidate behavior.) This discussion develops two themes: first, that campaign practices can be subjected to normative evaluation and second, that the legitimacy of public decisions with respect to a particular theme requires a give and take in public discourse pertaining to that theme. I conclude by discussing dialogue, noting that the presence of dialogue would entail a shift away from the less beneficial communication driven by self-interested candidates toward a more constructive discourse that I liken to a political conversation. I begin with some observers who have remarked on the absence of dialogue in political campaigns.

Pundits have routinely condemned the state of public campaigning since the founding of the United States. Perhaps the greatest burst of criticism occurred following the advent of television broadcasting when Kelley (1960) authored the first comprehensive review of campaign discourse. He began by saying, "the character of political campaigns in the United States has been a continuing source of dissatisfaction to friendly students of American political life" (Kelley 1960, p. 1). His statement of the problem was pithy: "the discussion found in campaigns tends to impair the judgment of the electorate and to upset the formulation of coherent public policies" (Kelley 1960, p. 2). If anything, the situation has worsened in the ensuing years. Aside from an ever-present stream of criticism and schemes for reform, the lack of campaign substance is as glaring to contemporary observers as it was to Kelley almost half a century ago.

If there is one uniquely distressing feature of campaigns, it seems to be the tendency for candidates to talk past each other. James Bryce observed this phenomena – as early as 1890.

> Anyone who should read the campaign literature of the Republicans would fancy that they were opposed to the Democrats on many important points. When he took up the Democratic speeches and pamphlets he would again be struck by the serious divergences between the parties, which however would seem to arise, not on the points raised by the Republicans, but on other points which the Republicans had not referred to (Bryce, cited in Kelley 1960, p. 61).

In their now classic study of electoral behavior, Berelson, Lazarsfeld, and McPhee noted the same pattern in the presidential election of 1948: "The opposing candidates tended to 'talk past each other' almost as if they were participating in two different elections. In that respect, there was little meeting of the minds or joining of the issues between [Thomas] Dewey and [Harry] Truman on many major topics. Each candidate stressed the matters considered most strategic and effective in his own propaganda" (Berelson, Lazarsfeld, and McPhee 1954, p. 236). More recently, Petrocik (1996) and Sellers (1998) have documented the validity of this generalization insofar as contemporary presidential and senatorial campaigns, respectively, are concerned. I argue that it is this tendency of candidates – to focus on self-serving themes and avoid constructive engagement – that impairs the functioning of campaigns as political institutions.

Critics hold firm, and generally uncontroversial, ideas about what the campaign should accomplish. Kelley argued that "the politician should owe his office to his ability to persuade an informed electorate of his qualifications for office and the wisdom of his policies, and to that ability alone. He should not be able to win and maintain power because he could buy or manufacture votes" (Kelley 1960, p. 1). Anyone who possesses a degree of faith in electoral institutions would agree. Many democratic theorists go even further, holding that the constructive conduct of the campaign is vital to the polity. "The quality of the making and of the defending of claims in the public sphere can be seen as a measure of society's success" (Kingwell 1995, p. 83). For instance,

Fishkin (1992), among others, argues that public deliberation is necessary to establish the legitimacy of public decisions.

In the following sections, I examine campaign discourse from the perspective of democratic theory, articulate some characteristics of the ideal discourse envisioned by theorists, and propose dialogue as a normative standard consistent with that ideal. I begin with the claim that it is proper to evaluate political campaigns from a critical standpoint. Some theorists, as well as the less philosophically inclined, dismiss contemporary campaigns as shams, unworthy of normative evaluation. Nevertheless, substantial critical discussion of campaigns occurs. In my view, this criticism should build from existing literatures on public deliberation, so long as the idiosyncratic features of campaign discourse are kept in mind. The essential tenet of this literature is that vigorous public debate is necessary to the health of a democratic society. My argument turns on the putatively central location of campaign discourse in such debate.

THE NORMATIVE EVALUATION OF CAMPAIGNS

To the casual observer it seems common for political theorists to dismiss the United States' formal electoral processes. After all, to caricature this view, these spectacles should not be taken as anything but evidence that the existing system is beyond reform. Politicians are craven and say anything in single-minded pursuit of office; therefore, they produce discourse devoid of real meaning. Voters appear foolishly optimistic or ignorant, being bamboozled time after time by the same political tricks. The media provide the usual horserace coverage – pointless and dull to anyone other than the dedicated fan. Moreover, the campaign is only tenuously linked to public policy, which itself seems remote from the issues most theorists confront. Nevertheless, the subject of reform continues to be discussed seriously; prominent theorists often offer suggestions and promote projects with reform in mind. Rawls, for instance, clearly includes "the discourse of candidates for public office and their campaign managers, especially in their public oratory, party platforms and political statements" in his specification of the "public political forum" (Rawls 1997, p. 767). However, most of these efforts, as I will discuss, are small in scale, of dubious utility, or focused on alternative forums.

In contrast, all theorists take notions of civil society and the public sphere quite seriously. The question of what conditions enhance public discourse and the health of society is receiving increasing attention under the heading of deliberative democracy. Building from these efforts, I apply the language and logic of democratic theory to discuss the messages sent in political campaigns. My concern is not with the precise definitions of the public sphere or other nuances; rather, I rely on broadly applicable notions, such as legitimacy and the proper conduct of public discourse. Instead of dismissing the campaign as an unredeemable institution, we should judge and reform campaign discourse using standards that apply to all public discourse, keeping in mind the general point made by detractors. They argue, at the least, for lowered expectations as to what reform can accomplish.

Campaigns, understood as forums for public deliberation, seem too valuable to be written off. Society needs healthy communicative institutions, and the campaign has attractive features from the standpoint of supporting public speech. Campaigning receives the lion's share of the United States's distinctly political communication resources. These resources would be better spent in an exercise that contributed to the public well-being beyond the selection of a particular candidate for office. Citizens (as well as journalists) have been socialized into paying more attention to the campaign than to any other political events. For example, while certain issues or events may temporarily garner interest, no national event will receive the regular attention garnered by the presidential election.

In keeping with the design of our system of government, politicians also pay close attention to campaigns and electoral results. Their thoughts and actions are often informed by campaign activity although they might not be directly affected by the outcome. Officials and other elite communicators are also adopting the communications style that typifies campaign discourse. As Kernell (1988) argues, the officeholder has come to speak in the voice of the candidate even outside the formal context of an election. It is common to hear about noncandidates engaged in political persuasion attempts called campaigns, as in the campaign for health care reform, for example. In these efforts, political entrepreneurs take advantage of the methods used by regular candidates.

If the campaign is indeed an institutionalized forum that bridges civil society and the rest of government, then its health is critical. As campaign discourse channels the flow of discussion in civil society toward specific government offices, we would do well to evaluate it in light of the standards used to judge other public discourses. At a minimum, the more faithful campaign discourse is to these other discourses, the more the flavor of this broader discourse is extended and brought to bear on elected officials. Most important, the quality of campaign discourse affects the legitimacy of specific electoral decisions as well as the legitimacy of the policies implicated in the discussion of particular themes. This linkage is intrinsic to the notion of a mandate. The victory of a candidate associated with a certain program grants that program more authority in subsequent formal processes. For these reasons, the potential of the campaign as a discursive institution should be taken seriously.

NORMATIVE THEORY ON PUBLIC DISCOURSE

With the provisional acceptance of the campaign's suitability for normative evaluation, principles imported from democratic and critical theory lead to the acceptance of dialogue as a minimal standard for discourse. To preview, Habermas (1982, 1985, 1996) claims that members of our society intuitively commit to an ideal when they communicate. This ideal contains criteria that can be used to render judgments about the quality of a particular discourse. In addition, since an approximation of this ideal in public discourse is a prerequisite of legitimate governance, the explication of these principles underlines the importance of campaigns as discursive institutions. My first step is to briefly retrace Habermas's conclusions concerning communication practices and democratic society. However, specifying a more precise relationship between public discourse and the successful functioning of our democracy requires more, so I include observations and ideas originated by other democratic theorists, especially those recognized as proponents of deliberative democracy.

Habermas (1982, 1985, 1996) concerns himself with the institutional possibilities of realizing a democracy centered on a procedure of free, public deliberation (O'Neill 1997). To oversimplify, the construction of an ideal for public deliberation constitutes his work and then motivates proposals for standards and reforms. Like Scanlon (1982), Rawls (1993, 1997), and other democratic theorists, Habermas argues that reasoning is central to the proper conduct of social and political life because we, as human beings, desire, expect, and produce justifications for our actions. Habermas links the employment of reason to human communication. This linkage parallels Rawls's ideal of public reason, which is:

> Realized or satisfied whenever judges, legislators, chief executives,
> and other government officials, as well as candidates for public

office, act from and follow the idea of public reason and explain to other citizens their reasons for supporting fundamental political positions in terms of the political conception of justice they regard as the most reasonable (Rawls 1997, p. 768).

Habermas's method, however, differs because he pursues the explication of the ideal through an analysis of human communication, which he calls "discourse ethics."

Habermas develops the concept of communicative rationality as the cornerstone of his project. Political theory often implicates rationality but Habermas uniquely emphasizes discursive behavior. He claims, albeit not uncontroversially (see Manin 1987, for a critique of this distinction), that communicative rationality is distinct from strategic or instrumental behavior. Strategic rationality, which frequently appears in everyday behavior, including speech, is characterized by its orientation toward satisfying narrow self-interest. Communicative rationality, in contrast, follows Kant's premise that human beings are autonomous ends and, therefore, entitled to respect without regard for their "utility" (Reiss 1970). It incorporates this respect as it focuses on reaching social agreement through a process of reason-giving, reaching understanding, and uncoerced persuasion. Thus, Habermas places communicatively rational discourse above calculation, manipulation, or hot air – to borrow a term from game theory, it is more than "cheap talk" (Johnson 1993).

This concept is central because humans presuppose an ideal as we engage in rational (in the communicative sense) discourse. This ideal can be articulated in a set of rules governing the production of mutual understanding. Note that not all discourses need aspire to this ideal; rather, rational discourses exist like "islands in a sea of everyday practice" (Habermas 1982, p. 235). In other words, they are the exception to the rule of everyday communication, arising to continue communication in the presence of disagreement. It is this aspect that makes them so important because, in resolving disagreements, rational discourses generate justifications for principles of social and political justice. The examination of the ideal uncovers the procedures that successful resolution must follow. Thus, Habermas's examination grounds a universal criterion for political legitimacy within proper public deliberation.

Habermas and his adherents often employ complex terminology for concepts of legitimacy and deliberation, but the practical implications of his arguments in this domain are relatively straightforward. With this background established, I equate rational discourse with deliberation and move to discuss political legitimacy and Habermas's ideal despite that fact that this usage undermines certain distinctions. Some of Habermas's views are controversial, as well. His critics have argued that his view unnecessarily privileges the status quo by buttressing those already in power (e.g., Young 1990) and that his aspirations toward universality remain unsatisfied (e.g., Walzer 1994). Nevertheless, my payoff lies in integrating Habermas's work on public discourse with that of other scholars to move quickly toward the subject of contemporary campaigns.

LEGITIMACY AND PUBLIC DELIBERATION

Legitimacy is the preeminent concept in democratic theory. It is essentially a rubric for justice, a concept that corresponds to the morality of the state. Unjust states or policies can be said to be illegitimate and, in that sense, bad. In a democracy, and probably in all societies, legitimacy somehow derives from the consent of the polity to the government's actions. Popular sovereignty, the retention of ultimate power in the hands of the people, embodies this ideal (Dahl 1989). Taxes, for example, are legitimate because, in some sense, we have collectively agreed to them. Thus, the linkages between government and people are critical to the realization of legitimacy. Following another of Habermas's (1975) ideas, a dualistic notion suggests that legitimacy flows from civil society into the formal apparatus of the state. Therefore, the legitimacy of a particular taxation regime depends on many contextual and procedural factors. Much of democratic theory can be seen as investigating the conditions of this flow. Of particular relevance is the work associated with the concept of deliberative democracy.

Many scholars have claimed that public deliberation is a vital and beneficial feature of democracy (Mansbridge 1980; Barber 1984; Cohen 1989; Fishkin 1991, 1992; Gutmann and Thompson 1996; Page 1996). Their logic builds directly on Mill's (detailed in Robson 1977) notion of a marketplace of ideas. Free speech makes for collective decisions that are based on better premises than otherwise possible; thus open public debate leads society closer to truth than otherwise possible. Greenawalt (1989) enumerates other potential benefits. The legitimization of government promoted by public expression stabilizes the polity. Access to the public sphere permits dissatisfied segments of society to air their grievances, releasing tension. It may be argued that freely allowing such dissent is risky, however, it seems to lead to increased cohesion over time. In general, universal access to the public sphere also confirms communal solidarity and promotes societal integrity.

Fishkin (1991, 1992) presents perhaps the clearest statement of the linkage between legitimacy and deliberation. Like others, he equates popular sovereignty and majority rule. Fishkin moves further by distinguishing simple majorities from "deliberative majorities," arguing that only the latter confer legitimacy on government action. A simple majority reflects the public's naive preferences. According to Fishkin, this is not sufficient. A poll question showing that a majority of citizens favored a progressive tax scheme, or even a referendum, in which that majority voted for one side, would not guarantee this decision's legitimacy. Deliberative majorities, in contrast, form in the crucible of public debate, so only they can be said to authentically represent the public's will. To draw a medical analogy, consider the notion of informed consent. The validity of a patient's agreement to undergo surgery is subject to question if it is not preceded by educated thought. In the same way, public decisions, including elections, are suspect if they are not accompanied by satisfactory discourse. In this sense, Fishkin (1991, 1992) mandates a collective informed consent.

This kind of distinction between legitimate and illegitimate majority rule appears commonly in contemporary democratic theory. In the first place it seems to reflect widespread intuitions about good decision making. As Shane O'Neill points out:

> It is not the sheer numbers which support the rationality of the conclusion, but the presumption that if a large number of people see certain matters a certain way as a result of certain kinds of rational procedures of deliberation and decision making, then such a conclusion has a presumptive claim to being rational (O'Neill, 1997, p. 33).

Similarly, Bessette (1994) refers to two voices in a democracy: "one more immediate or spontaneous, uninformed and unreflective; the other more deliberative, taking longer to develop and resting on a fuller consideration of information and arguments." Without deliberation, majorities are like mobs; deliberative majorities are qualitatively superior, having formed over time in the crucible of civil society. Bessette (1994, p. 35) argues that only this latter majority is fit to rule.

In general, then, the legitimacy of democratic government depends on public deliberation. This observation begs for a more precise definition of deliberation. Deliberation is a goal-oriented discursive process, involving reasoning and discussion over the merits of public policy (Page 1996). According to Rawls, "when citizens deliberate they exchange views and debate their supporting reasons concerning public political questions" (Rawls 1997, p. 771). It is not a series of preference expressions; instead deliberation is a process of will formation. Woodrow Wilson called deliberation "a living thing made out of the vital substance of many minds . . . and it can be made up only in the vital contacts of actual conference, only in face to face debate" (cited in Bessette 1994, p. xii). Essentially, deliberation is unconstrained debate mated to a process of collective reasoning.

The question of who deliberates, as Page (1996) asks, is equally vital. The founders believed that public deliberation would occur in the representative institutions of government, principally Congress (Bessette 1994, p. 35). Page answered his question by observing that our society divides the labor of deliberation, leaving it principally in the hands of the mass media. On the other hand, the majority of theorists would claim civil society, that part of the public sphere separate from more formal state institutions, is the locus of most important public deliberations. Because of this fact, theorists routinely call for a revitalized public sphere featuring vigorous debate. Beyond these calls, scholars focus on the mechanics of deliberation, which Habermas has done with respect to rational discourse. Specifically, he contributes a vision of the ideal, which is, again, presupposed by all that participate in rational discourse.

Habermas outlines perfect deliberation, what he calls the "ideal speech situation," to set some guidelines for actual deliberation. Habermas observes that participants in discourse continuously render judgments about the quality of form and content. Successful judgments, especially as to form, embody rules that taken together demarcate ideal speech (deliberation). According to Chambers (1996), Habermas specifies at least two conditions that must be realized to reach mutual understanding: first, participants must speak the same natural language with the same conventions, and second, communicative rules must presume that the participants desire to really agree. This example signals that Habermas (like Rawls and others) is a proceduralist, attempting to justify political norms by looking at their origins as opposed to pre-

senting a direct case based on their political content. Their normative force, then, stems from specific formation constraints. Here,
Habermas's procedures represent second order principles that apply to
deliberation.

Deliberative majorities arise in the give and take of public debate.
Claims are advanced, challenged, and elaborated upon in an iterative
and interactive process of consensus development. When a numerical
majority of members of society has reached consensus with respect
to a question, then a deliberative majority has formed. The distinguishing feature of a deliberative majority is that the consensus
accounts for the preferences of those not in the majority. Specifically,
Fishkin (1992) claims that legitimacy involves the airing of views across
all cleavages, requiring that every view be articulated. His examples
are limited to gender and race, but the notion of a significant cleavage
can be extended to any discussion area. A society may differ over income
tax policy, for instance, with some members supporting a flat-tax
while others favor more progressive regimes. The adequate representation of both views in public discourse is the critical determinant of
legitimacy. Thus, the distinguishing feature is procedural: the debate
leading to consensus is open to all speakers, who must participate in
some sense.

It should be clear that there could be many deliberative majorities
simultaneously, each on its own topic. In a pluralistic society, there are
many divergent viewpoints that for the foreseeable future will probably
rule out the kind of complete consensus that a singular deliberative
majority would require. Perhaps there exists a nascent deliberative
majority built around the basic operation of our government in the
sense of Rawls's (1971) "overlapping consensus." However, at the level
of everyday politics, Arrow (1951) and others have demonstrated the
fragility of majority rule. With even small numbers of voters, there is
no straightforward way to translate the jumble of individual preferences
into a single collective choice while satisfying a set of seemingly uncontroversial conditions, including majority rule. Instead, majority rule is
(at least theoretically) associated with "cycling" – the continual over-
turning of choices preferred by existing majorities in favor of choices
preferred by new majorities (Knight and Johnson 1994).

To summarize, legitimate governance requires a series of deliberative
majorities each having reached a consensus with respect to a particular
decision and context. Keeping in mind the number of decisions

government makes, not all are worthy of the full deliberative process. However, the legitimacy of any single choice is ultimately tied, albeit indirectly, to the amount of considered public support it possesses. Most important, the quest for legitimacy is a dynamic ongoing process that depends on the quality of public discourse.

CAVEATS PERTAINING TO CAMPAIGN REFORM

Given the importance of public discourse and its widely perceived problems, some scholars have naturally offered ideas for reform. In this section, I discuss their proposals, dividing them into two categories. First, I will discuss the mediational approaches suggested by scholars who are concerned with the general application of Habermas's theory, especially the maintenance of theoretical integrity. Our intuitions about candidates, nevertheless, suggest that these ideas do not comport well with the reality of contemporary campaigns. I argue that two features of the campaign – the privileges afforded to candidates as speakers and the candidates' zealotry with respect to their positions – effectively eliminate any prospect for successful mediation. Then, I turn to more pragmatic schemes for enhancing contemporary political campaigns. I argue that the pursuit of these efforts will likely be more fruitful, but that they will generally be drowned out by candidate communication in the status quo. On balance, these alternative ideas are wanting, so I move to my discussion of candidate communication itself.

Notions of reform reside beneath most theoretical arguments. Habermas (1996), for example, expresses faith in articulating the proper rule of law and developing legal measures to neutralize interference with ideal discourse conditions. In his vein at least three scholars – Dryzek (1990), Chambers (1996), and O'Neill (1997) – have offered examples advanced from clear explications of Habermas. The problem common to their ideas is that the social facts from which they work are too remote from mass political campaigns. This gap between theory and actuality often leads to the disfigurement of theory, much to the dismay of the theorist. On the other hand, rigorously sticking to theoretical commitments can limit prospects for success or the scope of potential applications. These scholars generally recognize this fact, so they have severely limited the scope of their discussions despite theoretical claims to universality. A review of their work also highlights some obvious features of campaigns that can act as impediments to reform.

All three scholars make detailed introductions of Habermas's logic concerning ideal speech to the everyday world of politics. In general, they advocate the settlement of political disputes through the creation of mediation settings resembling the ideal speech situation. In these situations small groups of participants may reach a consensus over their differences and identify the route toward resolution. Dryzek (1990) goes the furthest in this regard in his analysis of international negotiations. Undoubtedly his work is useful insofar as it applies to small group discourse. However, although theoretically orthodox, his overall reasoning affords little to the scholar of mass politics because of differences in scale and the nature of the discourse.

Chambers (1996) and O'Neill (1997) also offer rigorous explications of Habermas in the service of resolving political disputes via discourse. The cases they select afford us a view of the kind of situations in which they are interested. Chambers investigates the Quebecois separatist crisis in Canada while O'Neill focuses his attention on the situation in Northern Ireland. Their remedies are similar, revolving around the realization of an ideal speech situation on a large scale, which would generate consensus. They are particularly interested in the dynamics of perspective taking, arguing that combatants must reason together after acknowledging the validity of everyone's point of view. Over time, open discourse produces insight into the exact nature of the disagreement. This insight promotes the adoption of a proposal for resolution, a modus vivendi acceptable to both sides. Quite obviously their discussions range far from the concerns of scholars of contemporary campaign discourse.

There are some notable differences between campaign discourse and other kinds of civil discourse, which would-be reformers must take into account. Two points need to be addressed: candidates are not fully rational in Habermas's communicative sense and elections do not resemble the ideal speech situation or other mediational settings. Most theory relevant to discourse ethics subscribes to the belief that the force of the better argument will prevail, by definition, in rational discourses (Habermas 1984). Therefore, communicative rationality entails a principled responsiveness to arguments, a willingness to be criticized, assent to better arguments, and correct mistakes (Chambers 1996).

Major party candidacies regularly violate communicatively rational principles. Due to the processes underlying their selection, as well as the performance of their task, candidates are never really expected to accede to the "unforced force" of the better argument. While candidates may often agree with their opponents, seldom are they expected to change a publicized position, especially in response to an opponent's argument. Chapter four demonstrates the self-interested logic of this behavior. When a candidate does change positions, he or she is usually penalized for flip-flopping or being indecisive – attributes long considered to be flaws in those who seek elective office. Thus, candidates are necessarily zealots; they rigorously advocate their positions and never recognize the superiority of other views. On the positive side, we do expect candidates, in their role as propagandists, to present viable reasons for taking the positions they publicize. In fact, as zealots, candidates could be performing a public service by providing information in the conduct of their debate. The point is that the benefits of engaging in communicatively rational behavior tend not to accrue directly to the candidates. Candidates, as they stand, appear to have little incentive to be communicatively rational; rather, it is more reasonable to expect that the interactions between candidates aspire to this ideal.

In addition, the candidate is a unique type of participant in the public sphere. In response to critics, discourse theorists have made the equitable distribution of communication resources and opportunities a necessary condition for rational discourse. Depriving any participants of reasonable voice is anathema to all deliberative democrats. For instance, Bohmann (1996) includes equality of communicative resources as a critical condition. The reality of contemporary campaigns radically differs. By virtue of their role, candidates have an extraordinarily privileged voice. The candidate has a much greater ability to send messages and to command attention than does the ordinary citizen. By virtue of their access to funds and the media, the candidates jointly hold a monopoly over the decisive share of communication resources. This monopoly does not arise from declaring a candidacy. Third-party candidates, save exceptional cases, also lack the communicative power accompanying major party nomination. This skew in resource distribution enables candidates to selectively engage topics, knowing that, with the exception of their major opponent, others commonly lack the volume necessary to compete effectively in this critical choice. The net effect of this privileged access is to limit the number of serious interlocutors in campaign discourse, constructing, in Edelman's (1988) phrase, "the political spectacle." In short, all but a miniscule number of the polity are members of an audience instead of full discourse participants.

Scholars are aware of these points and have developed suggestions for reform that move beyond the mediational metaphor. Some important work foregoes the idea of mass deliberation in favor of more specialized deliberative organs. These scholars agree with the deliberative democrats that public discourse in the status quo is not satisfactory, but they limit the scope of reform to more elite institutions. Besette (1994) places the locus for public deliberation within the legislative branch of government, as noted above. Page (1996) argues that the mass media – the fourth branch – has the responsibility for ensuring adequate public deliberation. Thus, their reforms call for a division of labor, leaving deliberation out of the average citizen's hands. Given the complexity of government and the number of potential participants in society, these claims have merit. However, the fundamental link between the public's will and legitimate governance simply requires more public participation in deliberative processes.

Deliberative democrats generally agree that mass participation in deliberation is critical. In this vein, other scholars have advanced reform proposals that focus on creating alternative venues for mass deliberation. Rainey and Rehg (1996) advocate establishing a "Corporation for Public Interest Speech and Debate." Recognizing the massive disparities in communication resources that limit the participation of average citizens in public affairs, they argue for subsidizing public communication through an entity modeled after the public broadcasting system. Fishkin (1991, 1992) has perhaps the idea friendliest to applications involving large polities, like the United States. He calls for "deliberative opinion polling." Essentially, statistically representative random samples of the public would convene to discuss political issues or meet candidates. They would deliberate and the results of their deliberations would be reported to the rest of the electorate. Ideally, the entire electorate would value their considered choices, absorb the relevant information, and vote accordingly.

These carefully constructed suggestions merit support. However, it seems unlikely that either alternative will capture enough resources and/or attention to seriously threaten the communicative monopoly held by major party candidates. It is the behavior of these privileged speakers that must be addressed to realize any hope for enhancing campaign discourse. I conclude this chapter by returning to Habermas's ideal and discussing dialogue, the criterion I advance for judging the messages sent by candidates in campaign discourse. After a definition and some examples, I allude to dialogue's attractive features from the standpoint of empirical research. Then I focus on its desirability as a starting point for campaign reform.

DIALOGUE: A STANDARD FOR CAMPAIGN DISCOURSE

How can calls for enhancing civil discourse be applied to campaign discourse, especially the behavior of candidates? The ideal of deliberation is an appropriate point of departure, however, importing the application of advice offered from a mediational perspective is undoubtedly problematic. Likewise, expecting candidates to engage in a formal debate, with well-structured time limits, claims, and warrants is likely to be less than fruitful, given the state of campaign discourse and the tendencies of candidates outlined above. Events called debates that occur in contemporary campaigns are often no more than structured press conferences. In a broader sense, debate simply requires a principled advancing and defending of claims. This broader definition motivates my argument for adopting dialogue as a normative criterion for the evaluation of campaign discourse.

To dialogue a candidate must simply respond to the opponent's claims as opposed to ignoring them. Discourse absent dialogue resembles a play with many soliloquies, each addressing a different topic. The unrelated clutter of contemporary television advertisements, switching abruptly from topic to topic with no transitions to establish their mutual relevance, is another good example. This absence is what Bryce (1890), Lazarsfeld et al. (1954), and Kelley (1960) are referring to in their critiques of campaigns.

Judging discourse according to this standard is relatively easy. Pragmatically, human communication is structured around trains of thought. Non sequiters derail these trains and so are easy to spot. In everyday life we view these kinds of disruptions as disconcerting or annoying, so that lay observers can see them without too much training. Providing the audience is paying attention, it is likely that candidates who talk past each other create a similar kind of frustration. As a practical matter, the presence of dialogue enables the benefits of free speech. For example, just as the practice of parliamentary opposition challenges majority party claims and leads to superior arguments, so does dialogue ensure a better public discourse. After a dialogue occurs, a position can be assumed to be more thoroughly investigated, better reasoned, and appealing to a broader slice of the polity, including those previously in opposition.

One characteristic of dialogue is uptake, the adoption of certain portions of an opponent's rhetoric into one's own (Bohman 1996). Uptake implies a better political position has been generated because the new position has responded to criticism. It is this feature that gives dialogue its legitimating power. Dialogue moves every candidate to speak to every controversial theme. Candidates who do not dialogue are necessarily silent on some controversial issues; this silence is not consonant with the goal of vigorous public debate (Galston 1991). Thus, the presence of dialogue goes some way toward guaranteeing the public airing of minority views that Fishkin (1992) holds necessary to the legitimacy of political decisions. Similarly, Chambers (1996, p. 61) claims that, "real dialogue tests our moral intuitions and is the only way to test our political institutions," so that, "without some constraints on public discourse people risk talking past each other and thus foregoing the possibility of legitimacy." If dialogue takes place free of strong manipulation, any consensus that survives is capable of making a rational claim on us (Fishkin 1992, p. 155). Thus, dialogue paves the way for deliberative majorities and legitimate democratic governance.

At the same time, dialogue is a minimal notion. It simply avoids the situation where candidates ignore and talk past each other. Dialogue, understood as acknowledging and responding to another candidate's rhetoric, is a first step toward meaningful deliberation. Nevertheless, it is an important step. Psychologists, for instance, have demonstrated that two-sided arguments are more easily comprehended and (for more engaged participants) are generally more persuasive. In addition, the presence of dialogue creates dissent, which is likely to motivate increased thought (Nemeth 1995). To take a journalistic example, consider the point–counterpoint style in editorials. Newspapers often place opinion pieces advocating different sides in a pressing political decision next to each other. The idea behind this presentation style is to allow each advocate to present as good a case as possible and then let the reader judge the merits of the opposing claims. To take a now historical example, consider the Fairness Doctrine imposed on broadcasters prior to the Reagan Administration. Congress legislated that owners of scarce media resources had a responsibility to air arguments from both sides of every public issue raised. While this policy may have had problems, it enhanced public discourse.

At this point it is appropriate to consider an argument that undermines any claim that dialogue is a necessary feature of campaign discourse. Imagine as is common in the status quo that the candidates construct campaign messages in which they do indeed talk past each other. Specifically, the democrat and the republican would each create a list of themes to discuss that would be taken as an agenda for action in the event that they won office. The agenda would be constructed strategically, that is, with an eye toward attracting the most support. The campaign then would center on mobilizing party and other supporters around each agenda. In this case dialogue would be unnecessary and the winning candidate could at the least claim a mandate for subsequent governance. In fact, this presumably is what often happens in the status quo and those who believe that the status quo is acceptable would likely find my argument for dialogue spurious. I naturally hope that the logic presented in this chapter would lead readers to conclude the opposite.

To conclude outlining an ideal for campaign discourse, I would propose an alternative metaphor for the conduct of electoral politics, a different way of viewing politics common to much of critical theory (Dryzek 1990; Mansbridge 1980). Many political observers tend to see electoral campaigns as a game. This view arguably derives from the mass media's horserace coverage, which promotes an adversarial view of the entire process (Gitlin 1983; Patterson 1993). The game metaphor has several characteristics that typify current thinking about the campaign. They are worth interrogating with respect to promoting public discourse. Seeing the campaign as a political conversation stands in marked contrast to seeing it as a political game. To suggest that a paradigm shift of this magnitude is an immediate possibility is more than admittedly suspect. My purpose here is to motivate inquiry into the dynamics of political campaign and highlight the importance of dialogue in that setting.

Under a gaming metaphor, politics is at odds with the polity's interests. The electoral game's objective is victory, so the aim of campaign discourse reverts to the manipulation of political speech to enhance the likelihood of winning. The relative success of each candidate is measured only in terms of a vote plurality with the losing candidate receiving nothing. The campaign becomes a strategic exercise as opposed to a sincere one. The game paradigm fosters a particular set of expectancies and structures our view of the nature of the enterprise. Candidates are seldom expected to make any substantive contributions to public discourse. Regarding elections as games tends to carry with it a static notion of rules as well. These rules tend to take on a life of their own outside of the immediate communication process. They have a deterministic flavor, which is, if a candidate does so and so, then such and such will invariably happen. In this way, the game metaphor empties the process of constructive meaning. Rules can become reified in a way that ossifies them with respect to any particular campaign, especially encouraging the polity to view the campaign's rules as fixed, inflexible, and beyond its control.

Viewing the campaign as a political conversation can attenuate these negative features. Imagine a system where campaigning revolves around contributions to an ongoing conversation (Grice 1975). Candidates would be expected to be good conversationalists. As Gutmann and Thompson put it,

> a deliberative principle of accountability asks representatives to do more than try to win reelection . . . In a deliberative democracy representatives are expected to justify their actions in moral terms. In the spirit of reciprocity, they give reasons that can be accepted by all those who are bound by the laws and policies they justify (Gutmann and Thompson 1996, p. 129).

In this view, campaign rhetoric includes making arguments and responses that would foster the public's comprehension of public issues and decisions, letting the public come to terms with them and adopting reasons as steps in the process of the formation of deliberative majorities. The success of each candidate would be tied to the dialogic contribution they make. Winning and losing the election would no doubt remain important, but the loser's effort would not be so thoroughly wasted. The loser's contribution and influence of subsequent governmental action could and should be substantial. The conversational metaphor also undermines the notion of static rules. The arbiters of conversational success would be the mass media or the public. This view stands in contrast to the simple determinism embodied in horse-race coverage. To see the campaign as a conversation is to see it as a dynamic, constructive enterprise in which candidates and the polity interact creatively to produce meaningful political discourse as well as to select the holders of public office.

A genuine dialogue between candidates would be a definitive move toward this kind of enlightening conversation. Again, comparing the campaign to a debate, candidates should put forward a case in favor of their election focusing on the themes and dimensions that they believe were critical to the polity's understanding as well as their own victory. The distinguishing feature of dialogue would be the responsiveness of the candidates to each other's arguments and choice of subjects. Candidates would not just talk past each other, they would engage certain claims and propositions with new claims, pressing their opponents on particular points. In this way, according to Lasch (1995), dialogue uncovers new information. If the usual pattern of debate is taken to be point and counterpoint, an identification of common views and dissonant views occurs, and questions are raised. If the answers are not provided, a search for new information begins.

Elections are critical to the functioning of democratic forms of government. Electoral institutions ensure that the values and goals of the electorate correspond with the behavior of officeholders. In addition, many scholars have recognized the general need for institutions whose functions are to moderate opinions and structure issues so that they can be resolved (Polsby and Wildavsky 1991; Sundquist 1973; Shepsle 1972). The combination of campaigns and elections that occurs regularly at many levels of government seems well placed to serve this role. However, as the introductory descriptions of campaign speech attest to, this institutional combination seems to falter particularly at the task that is crucial from the standpoint of democratic legitimacy. In a putative ideal world, campaign discourse would feature a dialogue between the candidates that would mean that the campaign and election would more closely resemble a deliberative enterprise. In this event, electoral decisions would more likely be made by deliberative majorities (or pluralities) rather than simple ones, so that resources spent on electoral contests would be put to a more valuable public use than they appear to be in the current milieu.

CHAPTER 3

Understanding Campaigns: Background,
Theory, and Methods

In this chapter, I present the foundations for a scientific inquiry into the occurrence of campaign dialogue. In the first section I discuss the recent history of campaigns focusing on the change wrought by the advent of television and sample surveys. The point of this discussion is to contextualize and to establish the importance of this study as well as the importance of treating the campaign as a holistic phenomenon. Next, I move to review extant understanding of the campaign, especially the so-called Michigan and Rochester schools and the notion of low information rationality. I conclude with a sketch of a theory of campaigns that forms the basis for the formal (game-theoretic) model in the next chapter.

Onlookers have been complaining about the quality of public discourse for quite some time. As I observed in the previous chapter, the ferocity of this criticism has not decreased. In the current milieu, however, the most common response to critics of contemporary political campaigns – that they have always been shallow and we can expect little more – fails to acknowledge the increasing need for substance. Not so long ago, party organizations, exemplified by the smoke-filled backroom, were the centerpiece of American politics. They served as a conduit for passing information as well as a means toward gaining votes. The party filtered and transferred information between constituents and elected officials, so parties were responsible for organizing and facilitating the communication between government and the public necessary in a complex democracy (Aldrich 1995; Sundquist 1973).

Recently, however, a cluster of political, technological, and sociological changes – especially television and the sample survey – has cleared the smoke, fundamentally disturbing this channel between the public and officials (Bennett 1992; Kernell 1988; Polsby 1983). This new mode of governance, known as going public or the continuous campaign, depends on the same techniques as campaigning and has replaced hierarchical labor-intensive political organizations with a small cadre of strategists, fundraisers, pollsters, and media experts (Kernell 1988; Salmore and Salmore 1985). Campaigning itself has changed radically. Known most prominently as candidate-centered politics, this new style of campaigning emphasizes media usage, especially television commercials, to the exclusion of more traditional mobilization techniques (Ansolabehere, Behr, and Iyengar 1993; Wattenberg 1986). At the same time the sample survey has made it possible to ascertain voter preferences in the absence of party organizations. These two technologies correspond to the two communication paths between candidates and voters discussed in the next sections. Overall the new techniques of campaigning have brought about a subtle but decisive shift in the character of our polity's interconnections.

In particular, this transformation has had profound effects on the production and dissemination of political information. The campaign organization is now elected officials' primary source of information about the electorate's political whims and will. In the world of media politics, candidates depend on their campaign experts and the information they produce to win elections and, then, to govern. The officeholders' political capital turns on mobilizing public sentiment as filtered through the campaigning lens. Similarly, the public has been forced to rely on the campaign, understood broadly, for its political information (Mutz 1992). As the torchlight parade and stump speech have given way to the pseudoevent and thirty-second ad, the media campaign is taking on more responsibility for the transmission of information and for governance. As tools of the campaign, contemporary parties filter and organize political information at the candidates' discretion. In short, the primary mechanism for compensating for a lack of campaign substance is disappearing while few alternative mechanisms exist to fill the gaps. Those mechanisms that do exist, such as the media and interpersonal networks, are often co-opted into the campaign's service. Accretion and default have left the campaign as the most prominent provider of political information; thus, in the current political milieu, superficial campaigns are much more likely to have a debilitating effect on the polity.

The media, candidates, the system of campaign finance, and voters have all been held responsible for the campaign's lack of substantive content. No doubt, the media seem to be a deserving target. Critics of the media point to its adversarial stance toward politics or to the emphasis it accords political maneuvering (the "horserace") at the expense of substantive coverage (Page 1996; Patterson 1993; Gitlin 1983). Naturally, politicians and their advisors draw fire. Their do-any-thing-to-win attitude, manifested in their use of selective truths and polemics, seems to offend civic values and debase public reason. "Going negative" – an effective campaign tactic – increases voter alienation and decreases political participation, for instance (Ansolabehere and Iyengar 1994). The system of campaign finance bears further responsi-bility, effectively denying some candidates the opportunity to be heard (Alexander 1992; Sourauf 1992). Residual blame generally falls on the voters. Apparently too apathetic to demand or to apply proper infor-mation, the quality of the electoral audience forces the campaign machine into a lowest-common-denominator mode which undermines substantive discussion. The evidence pointing to these suspects is sub-stantial and much of this criticism is merited.

These critiques while valid, nevertheless, miss the interdependence of these elements. Campaigns are institutions, meaning that the cam-paign's emergent properties render it distinct from a simple combina-tion of voters, the media, and candidates. Many factors contribute to the campaign's lack of substance, but to address the problem success-fully, the factors cannot be examined in isolation. In this chapter, through the lens of a holistic theory, I argue that the proximate cause of the lack of substance is the incentive structure facing the candidates. Changes in this incentive structure, brought about in concert by voters, the media, and the system of campaign finance, promise the quickest and most effective way to increase the substantive content of campaigns. This chapter's objective is to condense extant scientific research on cam-paigns to pinpoint the forces that produce dialogue – both candidates selecting the same topic to discuss. In particular, I outline a theory explaining candidates' choices of what subjects to include in their cam-paign communications. Given this theory, I use these literatures to provide the definitions and foundational relationships from which to construct the model of campaigns and candidate behavior presented in the chapter four.

THE SCIENTIFIC STUDY OF VOTING BEHAVIOR
AND ELECTIONS

For the past fifty years or so much of electoral research has revolved around the question: Do campaigns matter? The answer is yes, with qualifications – if mattering implicates the ability of – the campaign to affect voters' decisions and thereby determine electoral outcomes. Political scientists have discovered that relatively few background factors, such as incumbency, the distribution of partisanship in the electorate, and the state of the economy, will effectively decide most elections. For example, an incumbent Republican running in a Republican district in a time of economic prosperity will nearly certainly win. The influence of the campaign in such cases is not pivotal. Yet, when candidates are closely matched in terms of resources and other electoral prerequisites, or in cases when one candidate's campaign is dramatically more effective, the campaign's influence can be decisive. Studies conducted decades ago demonstrate the campaign's ability to activate and reinforce voters' political predispositions (Lazarsfeld, Berelson, and McPhee 1948). At the aggregate level, the campaign affects the certainty with which voters can place candidates ideologically (Franklin 1992), voters' knowledge about specific issues (Ansolabehere and Iyengar 1994; Buchanan 1991), the salience of particular concerns (Iyengar and Kinder 1986), and, under the aforementioned conditions, general electoral outcomes (Bartels 1993; Petrocik 1996).

Thus, there is now a consensus that campaigns exert at least a marginal effect on electoral outcomes; moreover, in all the research mentioned above, the magnitude of campaign effects consistently increases in elections conducted below the presidential level. This research generally spans a continuum ranging from entirely empirical to purely theoretical. The Michigan school of research stands close to the empirical pole. These studies of voting behavior associated with this perspective employ a psychological paradigm, which revolves around sample survey techniques. The other major scholarly tradition, the Rochester school, tends toward the theoretical. The literature associated with this approach relies largely on formal methods to investigate the behavior of presumably rational candidates. This tradition has also led to a new literature unified by its common interest in the effects of information, the "low-information rationality" perspective. Each of these three bodies of knowledge contributes to the foundation upon which my study rests.

THE MICHIGAN SCHOOL

The American Voter is the seminal work in the Michigan tradition. Using sample survey research, Campbell et al. (1960) approached voting from a social psychological perspective. Though shocking at the time, the portrait of voting behavior they presented is nearly as accurate today as it was over forty years ago (Miller and Shanks 1996; Smith 1989; Nie, Verba, and Petrocik 1976). Voters pay scant attention to politics and have little motivation to organize and apply what little information they possess. Instead, they rely primarily on partisan identification, a psychological attachment to one of the major parties, to organize and make their political choices. Interestingly, the relationship between this attachment and the vote has remained strong although the parties' role as political organizations has weakened (Miller and Shanks 1996).

A structured typology of all potential influences on the vote grew out of the Michigan research. Known as the "funnel of causality" (Miller and Shanks 1996; Niemi and Weisberg 1993), this scheme classifies influences according to the time between the onset of an influence and the vote decision. The funnel of causality separates long-term forces (dispositional), which shape an individual's political outlook (contact with his family's political traditions, for instance), and short-term forces, which are circumstantial and unique to a particular election (such as the state of the economy and the campaign). Dispositional forces are voters' prior beliefs, attitudes, and values – their prevailing political predispositions. Americans acquire a sense of party identification and related affiliations at an early age, and these psychological anchors remain with them over the their entire life (Jennings and Niemi 1981). In addition to being the most important long-term force, partisan identification can also moderate the effect of short-term forces. These more situational forces, including the campaign, come from the political environment, which is discussed further below.

The Michiganders' perspective (and its survey research paradigm) dominates the empirical study of voting behavior. Its foremost contribution is an exhaustive account of individual voting behavior in national elections. My examination takes advantage of this research, especially its predictive power. The predictive ability of the funnel of causality is impressive, explaining close to all of the variation in individuals' vote choice. Knowing a respondent's partisan identification and his or her stance on one or two important issues regularly allows pollsters to correctly forecast the votes of 95 percent of the electorate (Niemi and Weisberg 1993). This knowledge allows a relatively simple representation of voting behavior, which plays a leading role in my model of campaigns in mass elections.

Research in the Michigan tradition also trained a spotlight on the central problem of American politics, the dramatic difference between the stereotype of the democratic citizen and the reality of public participation. It underlined an important question. How can a democracy function with ill-informed and apathetic citizens? Compared to the ideal of well-informed and interested voters' selecting candidates based on their qualifications and policy preferences, this research presented a bleaker reality of citizens voting largely because of an emotional attachment to a political party as well as a few other considerations. This stark reality provided the impetus for new accounts of the functioning of mass democracy.

Political scientists have sought to answer the question that these scholars raised. V. O. Key (1966) and Anthony Downs (1957) provided the clearest way to reconcile democratic governance with relative mass ignorance. In his echo chamber argument, Key recognized that voting behavior is a function of candidates and political institutions. He argued that voters' decisions echo the voices they hear in the political environment and that the quality of the voters' decisions depends on the quality of the information presented. For example, researchers have long considered ideological voting to be qualitatively superior to voting that centered on a candidate's likeability (Sniderman, Brody, and Tetlock 1991; Converse 1964; Campbell et al. 1960). Key added the idea that voters could only cast ideological votes in an ideologically charged race. This argument has a great deal of intuitive appeal though it has yet to receive definitive empirical support. The most systematic attempt to substantiate Key's claim was conducted during the ideologically charged 1964 presidential campaign (Nie, Verba, and Petrocik 1976). In this race, researchers found that there was a stronger relationship between a voter's ideological outlook and the vote, but their attempt to attribute these increases to the political environment was hampered by a change in the format of survey research questions (Sullivan, Piereson, and Marcus 1978).

The general point raised by Key, namely the importance of the political environment in determining the quality of the vote, has not been ignored. The study of the political environment and its relationship to voting behavior has received increasing attention. Several studies have demonstrated the influence of the political context on vote choice. For example, in a study comparing four Senate elections, Westlye (1991) found evidence consistent with Key's view. He demonstrated that voters were more likely to engage in issue voting in high salience campaigns – those with richer information flows. There are more specific contextual effects, as well. Most important, issues that voters consider important or salient play a much larger role relative to partisan identification than other issues (Repass 1971). Salience is a product of the political environment, a point that is highlighted by research on media priming (Krosnick and Kinder 1990; Iyengar and Kinder 1987). This line of research provides a basis for viewing campaign effects, and is elaborated fully in the development of the model in the next chapter.

THE ROCHESTER SCHOOL

The seminal work in the Rochester tradition is *An Economic Theory of Democracy* (Downs 1957). As the title implies, Downs developed a broad theory of the functioning of democratic institutions from existing microeconomic theory. This work established the research agenda for forty years of formal inquiry into elections. In particular, scholarship in this area has developed powerful tools based on the premise that candidates and voters are rational actors. It has also contributed greatly to a revised paradigm, commonly labeled, "low-information rationality" (Sniderman, Brody, and Tetlock 1991; Popkin 1991). Downs's approach is discussed in detail in chapter four, but its theoretical contributions are germane to this review.

Downs's claim – that voters are rationally ignorant – dovetails neatly with the empirical findings of the Michigan school. Essentially, Downs deals with the same problem as Key (1966) from the other side of the coin. He argues that voters perform a benefit-cost analysis when deciding to vote. Critically, there is an infinitesimal probability that any one vote will matter in the sense of reversing a specific electoral outcome. Given this minuscule probability of producing a benefit, any cost from a political activity like obtaining political information is too high. Thus, Downs argued that the ignorance of the typical voter was not surprising, and he saw the reliance on party identification as perfectly reasonable. He also argued that it was up to the parties to provide the voter with appropriate political information. In his scheme, effective representation in the United States' extant political system grew out of the competition between the two major parties. Citizens justifiably pay little attention to politics. In fact, for all but a few, it is not even rational to go to the polls (Palfrey and Rosenthal 1983).

Researchers in the low-information vein have taken these insights a step further and attempt to specify the costs and utility of political information. They claim that if citizens do vote, it is commonly accepted that decisions could and, indeed, should be based on simple rules-of-thumb called heuristics (Kahneman, Slovic, and Tversky 1992).

Partisan identification can be seen as a heuristic. The logic of a party voting heuristic runs as follows: one generally believes in the Democrats, who have nominated a particular candidate for an office, so one will vote for that nominee. Just knowing the candidate is a Democrat, in this case, is enough to cast a reasonable vote. Retrospective voting is another powerful heuristic. As has been well documented, retrospective voters reward incumbents who perform well by voting against incumbents whose administrations are associated with economic downturns or major wars (Fiorina 1981). Thus, a simple perception of the state of the country is all the information necessary to cast a reasonable presidential vote. This insight in combination with Michigan research is sufficient to understand contemporary voting behavior.

The Rochester tradition has also made a signal contribution to the understanding of candidate behavior. Black (1966) demonstrated that candidates in a two-party race would do best to make appeals targeted at moderate voters. The intuition behind this conclusion follows from the dynamics of two-candidate elections where each begins with a base on either end of the ideological spectrum, leaving the moderates to decide the outcome. This median-voter model is detailed further in the next chapter.

Thus, three points can be drawn from these research streams and the half-century of scientific inquiry they represent. First, the behavior of the typical voter is heavily conditioned by long-term factors. Furthermore, these factors, notably the voter's partisanship and attitude on salient dimensions, can be measured and used to accurately predict the voter's choice. Second, after long-term forces have acted, the remainder of voting behavior is susceptible to the influence of the factors found in the immediate political environment. Chief among these influences is the information flow created by the candidates themselves. Third, a candidate will generally do best by appealing to the voters holding moderate opinions. These three findings underpin my theory of campaigns. In short, extant research articulates a view of voting, candidates, and elections that makes it possible to explain the general absence of dialogue and predict its unusual occurrence.

A THEORETICAL FRAMEWORK FOR THE STUDY OF CAMPAIGNS

Elections are complex social interactions, which defy attempts to create grand theory. They involve different kinds of actors with partially self-defined roles engaged in a continually evolving process. Yet, nearly every American election conducted above the local level shares several common elements, and these elements, as specified in the literatures outlined above, suffice to create useful theory. Elections turn on the interaction between candidates and voters. As proposed by the Rochester researchers, I assume that candidates are rational actors. Further simplifying their behavior, I limit my interest to their choices of what themes or dimensions to discuss in their campaign messages.

Following the Michigan tradition, I assume voters behave in a deterministic fashion. Votes are determined by predispostions, especially partisanship and, to some extent, the political environment.

Campaigning is the process of planning and executing activities in an attempt to win votes (Lazarsfeld, Berelson, and McPhee 1948). The campaign proper typically begins with the nomination of candidates representing the major parties. With an identifiable opponent, candidates and advisors busy themselves completing their plans, scrutinizing themselves and their opposition to uncover potentially useful information. Each has strengths and weaknesses, well-known to political insiders, determined in part by their reputation, record and, possibly, prior performance. The candidate starts with a certain base, typically 40 to 45 percent of the electorate, on whose votes they can count. The remaining swing voters decide the election. Therefore, after accounting for his or her partisans, the electoral battle tends to be fought at the margins with each candidate hoping to sway a relatively small portion of the electorate. Candidates rely on the transmission of information – by buying advertising or attracting news coverage – to achieve this goal. At this level, the campaign is a straightforward communication process, and message creation is the essence of candidate strategy.

How do candidates create their messages? They choose to discuss the set of themes that they believe will maximize their vote share, given potential public opinion and their knowledge of the dynamics of the race. The number of potential topics is theoretically infinite, as discussed below. The dynamic element makes describing campaigning as a straightforward process somewhat misleading. The appropriate framework for studying candidate behavior must stretch beyond the simple one-way relationship between message sender (candidate) and receiver (voter). Instead, candidate behavior is based on calculations anticipating two communication paths: The main path of messages candidates create and direct at the public, and another path moving from the public back toward the candidates. Figure 3.1 portrays these paths.

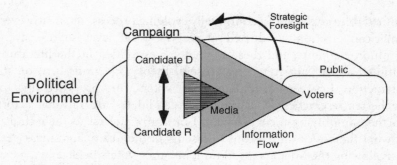

Figure 3.1 Conceptual model of campaigns and elections.

The main path is typically thought of as the information flow (Zaller 1992). It is the observable campaign, the advertisements, press conferences, and news reports broadcast at the electorate. Strategic foresight and feedback characterize the second path. Less direct and reliable, it represents the information that candidates glean from personal contact, polls, focus groups, and perhaps, intuition. The relationship between the two paths is recursive. Poll results and other information feed into campaign messages, which produce new feedback. To illustrate, pollsters take a benchmark poll, a snapshot of the electorates' attitudes at the beginning of the campaign. Using this snapshot, as well their experience, the candidates select the theme or set of themes that they think will put them in the best light with respect to swing voters. Orchestrating and disseminating the message consumes the majority of campaign resources. As it is disseminated, the message alters public opinion in ways pollsters can track. This may lead the candidate to alter the message, completing the loop.

To examine this dynamic, I freeze the messages voters send candidates, but they are important to understanding campaigns and the forces that produce dialogue. The public's original preferences and background information about the candidates are exogenous with respect to the campaign, and they are the independent variables driving candidate behavior in this theory.

Public opinion, in this view and in actuality, is an intervening variable because it causes and responds to the campaign. Critically, the structure of public opinion is endogenous (Stokes 1966). The contours of voters' cognitive maps change, albeit not drastically, in response to the campaign and candidate activities (Franklin 1994; Bartels 1993;

Popkin 1991). For my purpose, public opinion consists of a set of dimensions with each dimension corresponding to a potential campaign theme. A theme is anything a candidate can discuss that affects an individual's vote. Traditional issues, such as abortion or gun control are themes, as are less concrete topics. For example, if a candidate discusses an opponent's age and age becomes a consideration for some voters, then it is a theme. Questions of character, policy, or ideology may all be themes.

Themes can also grow out of latent attitudes that manifest in response to campaign rhetoric (Converse 1964; Key 1960). A feeling that the elderly are less competent, for instance, can be tapped and used to sway votes. My definition only requires that each dimension embody a unique distribution of the voters' preferences. This construction allows aggregation to bring some order to the chaos of mass preferences (Page and Shapiro 1992; Converse 1964). For analytic simplicity, I also assume these distributions are separable (one can divide any message into a discrete set of themes) and that they are independent (the distribution of opinion along one theme is not correlated with the distribution along any other). Neither assumption is necessary for the conclusions I draw, but each is arguably true (Converse 1964) and they substantially simplify subsequent discussion and examination.

To summarize, the public's original preferences and background information about the candidates lead the candidates to produce an information flow, which, at the margin, governs electoral outcomes. Returning to the age illustration, a bias against the elderly may affect the vote should one candidate be, in some sense, too old and the other candidate bring this fact to the public's attention. If candidates are the same age, the case for too old is harder for either candidate to make. If one candidate is too old, then the age of the older candidate is a potential weakness, well known in advance. In this way, candidates face an exercise in what Riker (1986; 1996) calls "herestethics," the art of persuasion through the manipulation of dimensions underlying the choice. The task of the rational candidate is to create the most effective campaign message by selecting the set of themes to discuss, which will bend public opinion most advantageously given the facts and existing predispositions.

This theory is admittedly simple, omitting what some rightly consider important features of electoral institutions. These choices narrow my project, making it manageable in addition to sharpening its focus on the factors governing the appearance of dialogue. Many omissions, such as the phenomena of voter turnout, preference intensity, and campaign finance can easily be added to the existing framework. Here, I will attempt to justify two other omissions. First, from my perspective, the mass media are a conduit of information carrying the candidate's message to the voter, so I do not model or analyze the relationship between candidates and the mass media. Second, I limit my analysis to campaign strategy understood as the selection of particular message themes. The model and analysis do not delve into subsequent actions on the assumption that campaign professionals create equally effective messages given the strategic choices of the candidate and top advisers.

Political reporting plays a minimal role in my perspective; the theory limits the media to acting as a carrier of campaign messages. Reporters and editors are professionals, but their incentives and therefore their behaviors are qualitatively different from those of politicians. Studies of news production support this view, though few directly examine the relationship between candidates and news (Gans 1979; Tuchman 1978; Epstein 1973; Sigal 1973). The sociological perspective developed in this research indicates that the actions of any individual reporter are highly constrained and so news reporting is largely a matter of routine. Reporters do try to fulfill their duties as members of the fourth estate, albeit tempered by these constraints. News people know that candidates control the information they supply. This knowledge can breed resentment, and the resentment increases as the manipulation becomes more outrageous or heavy-handed. For example, a collective view that George Bush's campaign in 1988 was able to profit from the use of misleading political advertisements led to the development of "ad watches." Ad watches examine the factual basis of candidates' campaign claims and have become institutionalized as central features of campaign news (Ansolabehere and Iyengar 1995). The upshot is that candidates must now anticipate the activities of the news media when they develop their messages. Lies and extraordinary exaggerations are usually criticized, for instance, so candidates avoid them.

Otherwise, campaigns are covered using the familiar template of the horserace. Strategic aspects of the campaign, such as poll results, finance, and the candidates' media strategies play a prominent role in coverage. Scholars (Patterson 1993; Gitlin 1983) have documented this frame and its associated pattern of coverage. This is not to say that the media cannot filter, distort, or amplify campaign message components, but the primary source for campaign news is the candidates themselves. For my purpose, the routines that the media follows means that campaign coverage will yield a predictable information flow given the candidates' behavior. In other words, the idiosyncratic coverage of any campaign issue or event by one reporter will invariably be counterbalanced across the entire campaign. Further, in a given electoral cycle, different reporters and editors provide the same general coverage of a given campaign. This fact frees this research from the cost of paying attention to the process that relates messages to coverage. I avoid analyzing candidate–media interactions; instead, I employ a "black-box" to span the gap between candidates and the electorate as shown in Figure 3.1.

I exclude the tactics of campaign communication for similar reasons. The choices responsible for the appearance of dialogue are the choices over what dimensions to include in the communication. Other choices, such as how to frame particular messages, are secondary to this consideration. The producers of specific message components make choices concerning which elements to address. For example, if strategy dictates that the campaign should discuss abortion, then the next step is to decide whether to focus on the right-to-life or the freedom to choose. These decisions do not affect the possibility of dialogue under my definition. I assume that candidates, on average, do equally well with these tactical choices, so I devote no attention to them.

RESEARCH METHODS AND DESIGNS

My research strategy consists of three steps common to all science: to develop an explicit model using this theory; test the model's basic prediction in a controlled setting; refine the model, and test it on a sample of cases in the real world. For the reasons outlined in chapter two, I have chosen to triangulate on the question of dialogue. Generally, I seek to develop and test a well-grounded understanding of candidate behavior and of dialogue in contemporary American elections. Following these three steps, I develop a game-theoretic model of campaigns. Second, I test the model via a case study of the 1994 race for governor of California, which employs experimental designs and, to a lesser extent, survey research. Third, I refine the model and test it on a sample of elections, using the technique of content analysis as well as survey and other data. In this section, I discuss the methodologies and my designs. Most of the specifics concerning actual procedures are saved for the appropriate chapters.

To begin the analysis, I investigate the absence of campaign dialogue using game theory because it provides a powerful tool for describing the behavior of rational candidates. A game is a mathematical model in which players individually make choices that jointly determine the outcome. The generality of formal models provide insights that go beyond those based exclusively on empirical methods. Models encompass the entire range of behavioral outcomes, including counterfactuals that may never appear in the real world. Assume, for instance, that it is not optimal for candidates to engage in a particular form of campaign communication (e.g., avoiding dialogue). As scholars, we would never observe such self-defeating behavior (unless it occurs by mistake), yet the presence of these possibilities may be critical to the explanation. By specifying the complete set of possibilities and identifying those that are most advantageous to the actors, rational-choice theory leads to holistic understanding and testable empirical propositions.

Formal methods have often been applied to the study of elections, however, few efforts explicitly model campaign activities. Many electoral models follow the pattern set by Downs (1957), typified by a unidimensional framework and flexible candidate positions. My model alters these features to make it possible to model campaigns and their effects more realistically. Given this depiction of voting and campaign effects, the model makes specific predictions concerning candidate strategy and the general look of campaigns. In essence, taking candidates to act rationally in their pursuit of electoral victory means that they will behave in predictable ways given an expectation of how voters will react to their campaign activities. The model predicts that the candidates will gain the most votes by emphasizing dimensions on which they are closest to the median voter. This comports with intuitions generated by campaign folklore as well as the volume of research stemming from the Rochester school. The more intriguing prediction, that candidates should ignore their opponents' choices, leads to an analysis of campaign dialogue and its prerequisites. Put starkly, the open debate often regarded as a mainstay of democratic decision making will never occur if candidates behave as the model dictates.

Dialogue has thus far been the subject of political theorizing, but not broad empirical scrutiny. The conventional wisdom holds that changing the subject is the best choice, a "dominant" strategy (Petrocik 1996; Budge and Farlie 1983). On the other hand, many political consultants argue that the candidate should respond in kind to rivals' initiatives. While this dictum is most closely associated with personal attacks, the logic behind it extends to all dimensions. The marketplace of ideas is assumed to correct false or misleading information. In the context of a campaign, not responding to an opponent's challenge may enhance its credibility. In this respect, these craven consultants are in accord with neoclassical democratic theory, which generally holds that an open and presumably two-sided debate is necessary for the public to develop well-grounded political views and establish the legitimacy of political decisions.

This prediction (and some related assumptions) is tested via a case study of the 1994 California gubernatorial race. Aside from California's size and its history as a setter of national trends, this particular race was chosen because the architects of candidate strategy made deliberate choices that are perfectly suited to this inquiry. Kathleen Brown, the Democratic challenger, chose to dialogue while Pete Wilson, the Republican incumbent, chose to avoid discussion of issues unfavorable to him. This election, therefore, provides a head-to-head contest of the opposing strategies, a critical test of the dialogue hypothesis. I am also fortunate to be able to draw on a transcript of a conference produced by the Institute for Governmental Affairs at the University of California at Berkeley. At this conference, principal members of the Brown and Wilson teams outlined their goals, strategies, and the calculations behind them in an open setting, attended by leading academics, journalists, and political consultants (Lubenow 1995).

The central element of the case study is a set of experiments conducted during the campaign. These were designed to assess the impact of campaign advertising on voters' choices. The experiments verify, in part, the psychological generalizations about voters, but more importantly, they provide a robust test of the dialogue hypothesis. In the first place, the experiment allows for the assignment of causality. Many factors, such as the media, external events, or voter predispositions, may have contributed to or even caused Wilson's victory. The experimental design allows the estimation of the specific causal role played by the candidates. The experimental approach also enables us to ask a vital counterfactual question. What if Brown (or Wilson, for that matter) had used a different strategy? The design I use provides an opportunity to estimate the effect of these alternative strategies and demonstrate the comparative disadvantage of promoting dialogue.

Some of the experimental results are corroborated with survey data. Because experimental designs usually employ a nonrepresentative sample of participants, their applicability to other settings is always subject to question. Sample survey methods provide a useful complement to experimental research because they employ a technique that virtually guarantees the validity of the results with respect to a particular population. In combination these methods identify causal forces and accurately capture the dynamics of this case.

The next part of this project is a broader look at elections in the real world, specifically, forty-nine U.S. Senate elections that occurred in 1988, 1990, and 1992. There are many valid scientific reasons to study these races (Franklin 1992; Wright and Berkman 1986), and chief among these is the availability of a large number of similar races that merited large but varied allocations of communication resources. This is one reason that the Board of Overseers of the National Election Studies decided to mount a special study of Senate elections. The first priority of this analysis is to establish the model's viability over a large sample, charting the amount of dialogue that appears in these campaigns. This analysis also provides the opportunity to confirm some of dialogue's beneficial effects. These cases also make it possible to refine the model and examine the presence of dialogue and the conditions that create it in everyday politics. The model generates several testable hypotheses which will be explored toward the end of the book. Some dialogue can be explained away as the irrational actions of certain candidates and those who make mistakes. Second, dialogue can be substantively important in cases where the campaign's psychological arena (public opinion) is effectively limited to one dimension, as in so-called critical elections (Burnham 1970) or when candidates can both make advantageous appeals to the median voter on the same dimension. Third, there are gray areas. Some discussions between candidates do not technically qualify as dialogue. These kinds of exchanges should be observed when candidates engage in thematic reframing.

This study employs an exhaustive content analysis, which is augmented with background and survey data. Content analysis is basically a technique for examining newspaper articles to recover the candidates' message choices. Human coders analyzed every article mentioning a candidate from one paper in each of these races. These data measure each race's level of dialogue as well as pointing out those dimensions on which dialogue occurred. The rest of the hypotheses mentioned above are then tested using a combination of this data and background information on the voters and candidates. In keeping with the theory, the candidates' positions on each issue and that of the median voter were scored using data from elite political sources, like the *Congressional Quarterly*. Finally, some auxiliary hypotheses are examined using survey data. These data were collected by the National Election Studies group.

CHAPTER 4

The Ventriloquist's Hand: A Game-Theoretic Model of Campaigns

In this chapter, I develop and analyze a game-theoretic model of campaigning in mass elections. My point of departure is candidate rationality; I assume candidates want to win election, so they act in ways that they believe will increase the likelihood of their electoral victory. More specifically, insofar as campaign activity is concerned, candidates choose to discuss the themes that they expect will maximize their likely share of the vote. I develop the model from a relatively simple representation of voting behavior, to which I add a typology of campaign effects. This typology consists of three effects: priming, learning, and direct persuasion, and so it includes all the social-scientifically documented effects of campaign activity on vote choice. By the end of this chapter, the completed model will identify the forces impelling candidates to resist dialogue. The model will also guide subsequent empirical investigations of candidate behavior and campaign substance that appear later in this book.

My approach diverges in three important respects from other formal models of elections. First, while candidates are understood to be strategic actors (as in other efforts), voters are taken to behave sincerely instead of strategically. I understand a vote to be the sum of a number of different considerations, weighted in proportion to their importance. This representation formalizes the well-researched psychological process underlying vote choice in which voters act in a nonstrategic fashion that minimizes the amount of thought needed to cast a ballot (Ferejohn and Kuklinski 1990; Fiske and Taylor 1991; Popkin 1991). Second, unlike extant formal models of the campaign, the model is multidimensional, consistent with the view of public opinion offered in chapter three. The political environment in which voters operate includes an infinite number of potential subjects, any of which can influence their decisions.

44

Finally, I assume candidates have externally determined, that is exogenous, positions on each dimension that are fixed for the duration of the campaign. I take these positions to be the common knowledge of voters and candidates. Taken together, these three modifications lead to a better fit between the model and the empirical literature on voting behavior, bringing the model closer to the actual practice of campaigns.

A game-theoretic model of the campaign in mass elections forms the core of this chapter. The fundamental result of this model is that message construction strategies that are dialogue-enhancing, in other words, which lead opposing candidates to discuss the same subject, are inferior or dominated strategies. Thus, the open debate discussed in chapter two, regarded as vital to democracy, will not occur if candidates behave as the model dictates. This result flows from the voters' utility function, which stems from the representation of vote choice and the typology of campaign effects. The function relates the candidates' choices to vote outcomes. As in economics, voters are more satisfied as their utility increases, so they select the candidate that they believe will provide the most utility. An analysis of this function identifies the likely actions of opposing rational candidates. In the first place, the model suggests how candidates select themes. Then, using game theory, I analyze the candidates' joint behavior to derive the proposition that rational candidates will avoid dialogue. (The formal work appears in appendix A.) This chapter's conclusion is refined in subsequent chapters because dialogue of some kind occurs in almost every election. I believe these refinements produce further insight into actual campaign discourse and lead to predictions as to when dialogue will occur.

I will also present experimental evidence to support some of my assumptions as well as the main result of the model. Some of this evidence is presented in this chapter in an attempt to establish the relative magnitudes of various campaign effects. The goal of this discussion is to ascertain the net effect of campaign messages, which govern the candidates' expectations as to how their communicative actions will affect their electoral prospects. Thus, these preliminary experimental findings help to ascertain which campaign effects are strong enough to warrant inclusion in a formal model.

OVERVIEW OF THE CAMPAIGN GAME

The strategic problem facing candidates in two-party elections is deceptively simple – the candidate who receives a majority of votes plus one wins. The situation corresponds to descriptions of coalition formation in a multiparty system (Laver and Schofield 1991; Axelrod 1970; Riker 1962). The candidate must pull together enough voters of similar minds to form a plurality. The important exception to this analogy is that, in mass elections, the battle takes place in a psychological space – the voters' minds. Instead of bartering among rational actors, the candidate faces an exercise in herestethics, the art of political manipulation via the transmission of information (Riker 1980, 1996). Candidates attempt to construct and send messages that will reshape the political environment to their advantage. The goal-oriented candidate wants the electorate to make its choice using a criterion based on a combination of dimensions favorable to him or her (Petrocik 1996; Iyengar and Kinder 1986; Budge and Farlie 1980).

In any campaign, there will be a range of themes on which communication can occur. Instrumentally rational candidates discuss themes they believe will maximize their vote share. These themes correspond to the dimensions of public opinion that candidates could integrate into their message. The candidate is only concerned with what themes to select, which equates to deciding the relative emphasis to give to all potential campaign themes in the message. In this model, the candidates perform no other action. The critical assumption is that a candidate's relative advantage along any dimension increases as his or her position moves closer to the location of the median voter's ideal point. Voters choose between the candidates by performing a weighted aggregation across all the dimensions.

The play of the game occurs in three stages. First, candidates face a distribution of voter ideal points and initial weights. Given this state of public opinion and their own fixed positions, the candidates must determine their optimal messages, and allocate their budgets accordingly. A candidate might, for example, expect that spending 60 percent of his or her budget discussing the economy and the remaining 40 percent on personal integrity would produce the largest gain in votes. These choices (along with other unspecified forces) determine the weight voters assign to the economy and personal integrity, as well as their knowledge of the candidates' positions on these dimensions. Drawing on their latent preferences, voters use these weights to decide the election. This scheme allows the campaign to be analyzed as a contest between instrumentally rational communicators.

Assumptions

My model is predicated on several assumptions, which I will discuss under five headings: candidate rationality, voting behavior, multidimensionality, fixed candidate positions, and symmetry. Treating candidates as rational actors is a prerequisite of formal analysis and seems reasonable given our knowledge of campaign techniques. The assumptions concerning voting behavior present voters as psychological actors and are consistent with the vast empirical literature on mass voting behavior. The assumption of multidimensionality is a departure from other electoral models, but it serves to highlight the priming effect (discussed below) and reflects a multidimensional conception of public opinion. Assumptions concerning all factors exogenous to the campaign are governed by the presumption of symmetry between candidates. Forces that can determine electoral outcomes, but fall outside the scope of my definition of campaign strategy, such as money, political skill, and the distribution of partisanship in the electorate, are assumed to affect both candidates equally.

CANDIDATE RATIONALITY. Candidates, especially those who run for higher office, tend to be professional politicians (Ehrenhalt 1991; Fowler and McClure 1989). Their progress up the political ladder depends on their ability to turn resources into votes. In an election, the candidate who makes this conversion more effectively, all else equal, wins. For many reasons, most notably protecting their livelihood, politicians engaged in a campaign go about the process seriously, giving it their full attention.

The shift from retail to wholesale politics has intensified this trend toward professionalism (Bennett 1992; Jamieson 1988; Wattenberg 1986; Polsby 1983). Previously the campaign was carried out by large groups of volunteers or political patrons who attempted to garner votes in small conversations. Door-to-door canvassing, candidate coffee parties, and rallies typify the more personalized nature of the pre–mass media political communication mode. Contemporary campaigns rely on mass communication; candidates, for instance, routinely use television to broadcast their message to large numbers of voters simultaneously. The success of contemporary campaigns depends on the effective use of modern marketing tools, such as polling, focus groups, and the testing of competing messages. Candidates have enthusiastically adopted these techniques, so that in the current milieu few sound bites are uttered that have not been thoroughly analyzed and pretested. Message creation is overseen by a legion of specialists, including consultants, pollsters, fundraisers, and media gurus (Salmore and Salmore 1985).

One upshot of the careful planning involved in developing campaign messages is that this aspect of candidate behavior can be analyzed from a rational choice perspective. Rational candidates have a clear over-riding goal – to win (see Wittman 1983 for a discussion of candidate motivations). They also have a well-defined set of options for doing so. The election turns on the creation and dissemination of a campaign message. Candidates approach this task rationally, selecting the best message in light of their goal. The decision over which message is best is not made haphazardly. There is a well-founded set of expectations on which candidates and their teams proceed. These expectations, the forces underlying them, and the actions they guide can be reduced to a set of propositions suitable for formal analysis.

VOTING BEHAVIOR. Voters, in marked contrast to candidates, are political amateurs. In general, they pay scant attention to politics and have little motivation to organize and apply what information they possess (Miller and Shanks 1996; Nie, Verba, and Petrocik 1976; Campbell et al. 1960). Some say that the typical voter cannot success-fully weigh the costs and benefits of going to the polls, let alone cal-culate the optimal voting strategy (Palfrey and Rosenthal 1983). Numerous attempts to prove otherwise have failed (Niemi and Weisberg 1993; Smith 1989). Studies have compared voters to candi-dates for local political office, for instance. Luskin (1987) found that even the most sophisticated voters were no match for even the worst candidates in terms of their political knowledge and their ability to reason through political decisions.

The issue at hand is how best to represent the voters' behaviors from the perspective of the rational candidate. Integrating the vast voting behavior literature into a singular coherent picture is impossible. On the one hand, the representation employed cannot be too complicated, but, on the other hand, it must capture the empirical flavor of mass voting. The compromise I offer characterizes voters' decisions as a simple psychological process. Voters are neither rational nor irrational. Votes are decided in a relatively deterministic way given a set of infor-mational and other inputs. Mass elections are contests in which ratio-nal actors compete before an audience of nonrational voters.

The specific representation of mass voting I offer adheres to a classic view of decision making developed by psychologists (Anderson 1966; Kinder and Sanders 1996). Voters are taken to make a decision by adding up each relevant consideration. Here, each consideration maps onto a dimension of public opinion and the aggregation across all considerations dictates the vote choice. The number of potential considerations is infinite. This representation allows the structure of preferences for a given voter to be wholly idiosyncratic. When summing across considerations, the voter weights each consideration according to its importance. If a voter believes the candidate's stance on abortion to be more important than the candidate's character, then the former receives more weight. Considerations that do not influence the vote can be said to have no weight at all.

I consider voting in the aggregate because that is how the candidate considers the electorate. Assuming voters are sufficiently independent, that is, no vote causes another vote, summing across voters yields the electorate. The electorate, like voters, retains a theoretically infinite number of considerations, but the chaos present in individual belief systems evens out (Converse 1964). The considerations continue to be weighted according to their overall importance to the electorate. Along any dimension, there is a distribution of voter preferences. This distribution can reflect crystallized attitudes or latent predispositions. Voter preferences can arise in response to campaign rhetoric (Jones 1994; Becker 1986; Stokes 1966; Key 1960). For instance, a remote feeling that senior citizens make bad officeholders can evolve into a consideration that sways votes because of the campaign discourse. From the candidates' point of view, the important feature of this distribution is the location of the median. So long as the expected median can be identified, it can be used to make strategic choices concerning the message.

MULTIDIMENSIONALITY. Nearly all electoral models follow the pattern established by Downs (1957). Building from Hotelling (1927), Downs compared political parties to businesses operating along the main street of a small town. He argued that parties, like businesses, want to be as close as possible to voters, their customers. Voters' preferences could be represented and ordered along an ideological continuum – liberal voters could be placed toward the left, moderates in the middle, and so forth. Intuitively appealing, parsimonious, and fruitful, this way of looking at politics has been at the core of electoral models. However, a single dimension generally does not account for mass political preferences very well. For instance, we know that voters' belief systems are not organized by ideology nor by any other single factor (Converse 1964).

Despite technical instability difficulties (Plott 1967; Arrow 1951), researchers have begun to turn toward multidimensional models. Enelow and Hinich (1982) first introduced nonspatial characteristics, like candidate personality, into a unidimensional model. Candidate reputation has been used similarly (Ingberman and Bernhardt 1985). Hinich and Munger (1994) move furthest toward a multidimensional setting; although they retain a reliance on ideology, their model employs a multidimensional space to represent voter preferences or "ideal points."

My model is also multidimensional. These dimensions are independent with respect to the distribution of voter preferences, meaning no dimension organizes or drives the preferences on any other dimension. While the result does not depend on this assumption, it greatly simplifies the analysis and reduces the place of ideological considerations in the model.

FIXED CANDIDATE POSITIONS. With respect to candidate strategy, Downs (1957) saw parties' activities as limited to picking the right platform or position. Black's (1958) theorem predicts that the positions of two parties in a unidimensional situation will converge toward the median-voter. This logic predicts and explains a large part of electoral behavior although actual candidates seldom converge to the same stance (Wittman 1990). This tension has motivated detailed examination of the dynamics of candidate positioning. The tradeoff between policy and electoral victory has been reconstructed as a tension between centrifugal and centripetal forces (Enelow 1992; Calvert 1985; Wittman 1983). Centrifugal forces push positions toward the extreme due to the need for support from activists and donors. The desire to win elections creates centripetal forces driving candidates to moderate their positions to obtain the support of voters close to the median. The exact balance of these forces depends on the goal of the modeling exercise.

I assume candidates' positions are fixed for the duration of the campaign. At one level, this assumption simply reflects empirical evidence, which shows that it is difficult to alter voters' perceptions of a candidate's positions. At another level, this choice reflects my particular interests. For instance, in some research the assumption that candidate positions are flexible is critical to investigating the veracity of candidates. Previous electoral models have identified the prerequisites of credibility: similarity of preferences, reputation effects, and penalties for lying (Austen-Smith 1990; Banks 1990; Ingberman and Bernhardt 1985). Seen from this perspective, the assumption that positions are fixed translates into assuming that candidates are perfectly trustworthy and consistent. I do not mean to say that candidates never lie; rather it is a matter of their emphasis that they don't. It should also be noted that it is unnecessary for messages to be fully credible or even to have a rationally discernible value in order to observe campaign effects. So long as campaign information alters voters' decisions in predictable ways, candidates can engage in rational message construction.

SYMMETRY. The model relies on several other assumptions, grouped under the heading, symmetry, all of which are intended to focus attention on campaign activity. The guiding principle behind this cluster of assumptions is to equalize candidates' access to the prerequisites for winning, such as money. Leaving aside motivations other than winning, candidates, as rational actors, would not pursue electoral victory unless there was a reasonable chance of success. This means that lopsided contests (a well-liked and well-financed incumbent facing an unknown challenger, for example) are not theoretically analyzable within the formal framework I offer. Symmetry also applies to other factors. In the real world, a candidate is often placed at a disadvantage because of voters' natural tendency to vote for their party's candidate. Frequently, the partisan balance of a district effectively decides an election before the campaign begins. I assume political skill, wisdom, and information are distributed evenly. Thus, the model concentrates on the choices the candidates make in a world where other electoral influences are held constant and equal.

A Typology of Campaign Effects

Specifying the way the campaign interacts with exogenous factors to affect vote choice is a necessary prerequisite to understanding candidate behavior and building a formal model. In this section I discuss my specification, which consists of three campaign effects – priming, persuasion, and learning. I define each of these effects, using a spatial voting model; then to illustrate further I present some experimental evidence taken from the 1994 California gubernatorial race. These data stem from a simple design, which compared subjects who viewed Republican candidate Pete Wilson's actual ads on crime to subjects who did not see the ads. Details of the experiential procedure are presented in appendix B.

PRIMING. Priming describes one effect of the information flow produced during the campaign. Priming pertains exclusively to the weighting of considerations in a given decision (Iyengar and Kinder 1987). If priming occurs, the more prominently a factor is featured in the information stream, the greater its weight in subsequent judgments. The idea underlying the priming effect is that the influence of the information flow is subtle. Rather than altering preferences directly, that is, within each dimension, priming presumes that the influence of messages on evaluation is indirect. In other words, the notion of priming highlights the potential for campaign messages to affect the relative influence of each consideration on the vote.

The ability of political communications to change the salience of considerations in the public's mind has been examined using experimental and survey methodologies. Analysis of National Election Studies data has shown that issues voters consider important or salient play a much larger role, relative to partisan identification, than other issues (Repass 1971). Studies of priming have demonstrated that the weighting of criteria employed in evaluating political actors is heavily influenced by the relative volume of each criterion in the information flow (Iyengar and Simon 1993; Krosnick and Kinder 1990; Iyengar and Kinder 1987). Researchers have applied the priming notion to elections, arguing that as the relative volume of information produced by the campaign along one dimension increases, its weight in voting decisions will also increase (Jacobs and Shapiro 1994; Iyengar and Kinder 1987).

In spatial terms, at least two dimensions are necessary to capture the priming effect. Imagine two themes, denoted x and y, and one voter, V, as displayed in Figure 4.1. Placing the median voter's ideal point at the origin, assume the voter weights each dimension equally. These assumptions generate a standard spatial voting set-up. Most important, in the upper panel of Figure 4.1, the voter's ex ante preferences (before priming) are Euclidean because the weights on each dimension are equal. For the sake of demonstration, the candidates are placed at $(-.2, -.5)$ and $(.5, .2)$, for the Democrat (D) and the Republican (R), respectively. By construction, the distances between each candidate and the voter are equal.

Now assume one candidate primes the electorate, changing the relative magnitude of the voter's weights. Assume, for example, that D is able to change the weights to $\frac{1}{3}$ for dimension x and $\frac{2}{3}$ for dimension y. The impact of the allocation can be seen in the new shape of the voter's indifference curves. As presented in the lower panel of Figure 4.1, V is now twice as concerned about dimension y as compared to dimension x, giving the voter elliptical indifference curves. The change

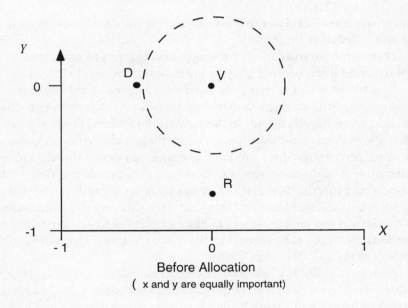

Before Allocation
(x and y are equally important)

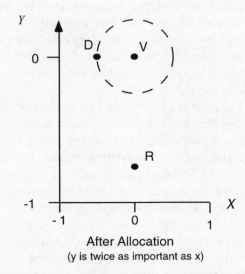

After Allocation
(y is twice as important as x)

Figure 4.1   The effect of D's unilateral allocation toward dimension Y.

effectively moves D closer to the voter, so that the distance between the D and V becomes smaller.

LEARNING (OPINIONATION). Learning generally refers to any increase in information levels because of communication (Hovland 1950). As used here, learning involves change in voters' knowledge of the candidates' positions. I will distinguish between two kinds of learning in this section, learning which leads to the formation of a perception of a candidate's positions, and learning which involves a change in an already formed perception. Both kinds of learning can occur directly or by inference. A candidate may, for example, delineate a position with respect to a specific theme, which voters come to know. Hearing that a candidate is a Republican or Democrat may also convey information. The partisan cue enables voters to place candidates to the left or right, respectively, of the position held by the median voter (Lodge and Hamill 1986; Palfrey and Rosenthal 1985).

Seen universally as a benefit of political campaigns, voter learning or education plays a role in all empirical campaign studies. However, the status of learning in voting behavior models varies. On the one hand, some voting models depend on intensive learning (Converse and Markus 1979; Brody and Page 1972). These so-called proximity models maintain that voters learn the positions of the candidates on every issue. In contrast, the low-information paradigm (Popkin 1991) holds intense learning to be too demanding in light of the known constraints on voters' cognitive resources.

The power of campaigns to change perceptions of candidate positions also figures prominently in rational choice models (Austen-Smith 1990; Banks 1990; Ingberman and Bernhardt 1985; Downs 1957). In spatial terms, learning refers to movement within a dimension. When learning occurs, a candidate's position relative to the median voter should change, however, actual observation of campaign effects tends to show that this kind of movement is not common.

Another kind of learning has received much stronger empirical support. In the absence of prior knowledge, campaign advertisements focusing on a particular subject lead to increased "opinionation," more voters being able to pinpoint that candidate's position with respect to that theme. This phenomenon is distinct from the first kind of learning, which presumes that voters already have an opinion. Under the first kind of learning, messages can change voters' perception of a candidate's position within a dimension. For example, an ad may lead a voter to believe that a candidate favored a more conservative position on public safety than previously thought. Thus, the first kind of learning is more akin to persuasion than to opinionation. Learning of the first sort has not been well supported; it is learning of the second sort that has received ample empirical validation (Ansolabehere and Iyengar 1994; Buchanan 1991; Popkin 1991).

DIRECT PERSUASION. Psychologists generally define persuasion as any message-induced change in attitudes or beliefs (Petty and Cacioppo 1986). Thus, in common usage, all campaign activities are persuasive. Finding out something new about a candidate, for instance, can be called persuasion if the new information changes vote intentions. (Intentions are what vote choice is called in the context of survey research, as in: Who do you intend to vote for in the upcoming election?) A narrower conception of persuasion distinguishes it from other effects, especially learning and priming. When used here, direct persuasion refers to the power of campaign messages to alter voters' ideal points. In the aggregate, direct persuasion refers to the ability of the campaign to move the position of the median voter relative to those of the candidates, for example.

Campaigns have demonstrated little ability to alter voter preference directly. In the aftermath of World War II, a tremendous effort was expended toward studying persuasive messages. These studies found that very little direct persuasion takes place during the campaign (Klapper 1960; Berelson, Lazarsfeld, and McPhee 1952; Lazarsfeld, Berelson, and Gaudet 1948). These early researchers concluded that campaign effects were limited to the activation and reinforcement of previously held beliefs. More recent research has also provided evidence to support this minimal view (Bartels 1993; Finkel 1993). In order to confirm these effects and illustrate the campaign effects more concretely, I will briefly present the results of a one-ad experiment. This experiment previews the techniques that form the basis of the next chapter and also serves as a baseline for the comparisons made later in the book. Again, the experimental protocols are presented in appendix B.

ONE-AD EXPERIMENTAL DESIGN USED TO VERIFY THE TYPOLOGY

This experimental procedure enables a direct examination of the model's assumptions concerning the effect of political advertisements. A one-ad design (see Figure 4.2) was employed to confirm premises conforming to the priming, learning, and persuasion effects developed above. In this study half of the participants (N = 82) were randomly assigned to see a videotape including a thirty-second Pete Wilson

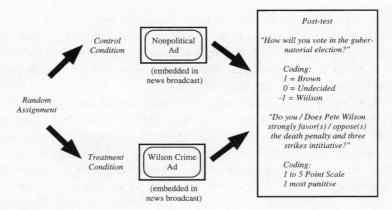

Figure 4.2   One-ad design.

commercial on crime while the other half were treated identically, with the exception that the Wilson spot was edited out and replaced with a nonpolitical commercial. The Wilson ad depicted his stance as tough on crime and emphasized his support for locking up violent felons. After seeing the tapes, all participants were asked how they intended to vote in the upcoming election; their answers were coded one for Kathleen Brown, zero for undecided, and negative one for Pete Wilson.

In the control condition, the mean vote was .12, meaning that if a "trial heat" between Brown and Wilson were held among these subjects, Brown would win by twelve percentage points (the results discussed in this section are all summarized in Table 4.1). Among those seeing the Wilson ad, the mean vote was −.12, meaning that Wilson *would win* a trial heat among these subjects by twelve percentage points. This 24-point swing between the control and treatment groups was statistically significant at the .10 level, $F(82) = 2.0$.

Why did the advertisement cause this shift? Following the typology of campaign effects developed in the previous chapter, the likely cause is some combination of priming, learning, and persuasion. In line with that discussion, we expect that priming and learning in the form of opinionation should cause the vote shift. To assess these predictions, subjects were also asked other questions charting their opinions and knowledge. For example, they were asked, "Do you strongly favor or oppose the death penalty?" Responses were coded on a five-point scale where one was the most punitive, five was the most lenient and three was a neutral response. Similarly worded questions tapped a subject's

Table 4.1   *Selected Results Concerning the Effect of Campaign Ads*

	Control	Treatment
Vote (Brown's advantage)	12%	−12%*
Priming		
(Relationship between crime attitudes and vote[a])	.02	.22**
Opinionation		
(% making placements of Wilson)	76%	95%**
Learning		
(Mean placements of Wilson)	1.63	1.64
Persuasion		
(Mean of respondents' own opinions)	2.52	2.77
N:	41	41

Notes: [a]OLS Regression estimates after controlling for the effect of subject's party. Asterisks represent approximate significance levels: **$p < .05$; *$p < .1$.

knowledge of Pete Wilson's positions and their attitudes toward the three-strike initiative. This initiative, also called Proposition 184, was a ballot measure that amended state law to require mandatory prison sentences for those convicted of three felonies.

Under priming, exposure to an ad featuring a particular theme leads voters to assign increased weight to that thematic dimension in reaching their voting decisions. Specifically, seeing the Wilson ad on crime should make subjects more likely to use crime as a consideration in determining their vote. Thus, the relationship between attitudes on public safety issues and the vote should be stronger in the treatment condition than in the control group. After statistically controlling for the voters' partisan identification, voters in the control group showed no relationship ($b = .02$) between crime attitudes and the vote. However, voters seeing the Wilson ad showed a much stronger relationship ($b = .22$; $p < .05$). Details concerning the estimation procedure can be found in the appendix B. These results confirm that the ad primed subjects' attitudes on crime with respect to the vote.

Opinionation describes the ability to make a judgment as to where a candidate stands on a particular dimension. As an hypothesis, opinionation predicts more people should be able to state where a candidate stands (using an issue scale) after exposure to an advertisement on that issue. Specifically, exposure to the Wilson crime ad should lead more voters to express an opinion as to where Wilson stands with respect to crime. Attitudes concerning crime were tapped using two indicators, measuring participants' feelings about the death penalty and the three-strike initiative. For the death penalty, for instance, the ads moved opinionation from 76 percent in the control group to 95 percent in the treatment group. Averaging across two questions, 23 percent more voters in the treatment group were able to express some opinion as to where Wilson stood on crime, a shift from 73 percent to 96 percent. This was a substantial and statistically significant change, $F(82) = 10$, $p < .01$. Voters were also better able to make placements of Wilson's opponent, Kathleen Brown. Less than two-thirds of the control voters (61 percent) offered an opinion as to where she stood on these issues while 81 percent of the subjects seeing the ads did so, $F(82) = 2$, $p < .05$. Thus, Wilson's crime ads led to a dramatic increase in voters' ability to say where both candidates stood with respect to that issue.

To examine learning, defined as changes in the perceptions of a candidate's positions, averages of the subjects' actual issue placements were calculated. In this case, the perceived locations of Wilson's stances with respect to the death penalty and the three-strike initiative on public safety were at issue. To register the effects of the increase in the level of opinions offered by participants seeing the crime ad, those not offering opinions were excluded from this part of the analysis. On the three strikes theme, the control group collectively placed Wilson at 1.51, very close to the toughest end of the five-point crime scale, while those seeing the ads placed him at 1.47. For the death penalty, the control mean was 1.74 and the exposure mean was 1.80. There was no statistical difference between those who saw the ads and those who did not.

The Wilson ads may have also affected the subjects' perceptions of Kathleen Brown's positions on crime-related issues. Similar ratings for Brown indicated only slight movement. Her mean rating on three strikes moved from 3.23 (control) to 3.33 (Wilson ad). On the death penalty, perceptions of her position moved from 3.60 to 3.78. Again, no statistically significant differences were observed.

Persuasion effects are closely related to learning effects except that they implicate voters' own beliefs concerning crime-related issues. Movements of voters' self-reported attitudes on particular dimensions would evidence the presence of direct persuasion effects. An ad on crime would persuade voters to be more favorable to the death penalty, for example. Stated as an hypothesis, the Wilson ad advocating tougher sentences and the death penalty should make viewers' aggregate position on crime-related issues more punitive. The ad caused the average attitude toward the death penalty to move from 2.52 in the control condition to 2.17 in the treatment condition. Attitudes toward the three-strikes initiative moved from 2.61 to 2.5. Averaging across the two issues, the mean of the treatment group was 2.77 compared to a control group mean of 2.68. With 69 subjects (divided roughly equally), this effect is not statistically significant, $F(69) = .79$. Though the ads seem to have moved the public slightly, the magnitude of the change was small. The experimental assessment of Wilson's crime ad confirms the absence of direct persuasion as well as of learning.

Summary Concerning Campaign Effects

A review of the literature demonstrates two specific effects of campaign messages. First, campaign messages seem to inform voters of the candidates' positions on the subjects discussed. To illustrate with the experimental results, exposure to the Wilson crime ad increased the number of subjects who were able to indicate where Wilson stood on crime-related issues. Second, campaign messages affect the importance of the discussed subject in the voter's mind. The Wilson ad increased the reliance on crime attitudes in reaching a voting decision. In contrast, campaign messages leave a much smaller trace where direct persuasion is concerned. Wilson's ad did not change the average impression of the location of Wilson's positions (or Brown's) nor did it persuade voters to change their own positions.

The one-ad design confirms the assumptions concerning the effect of political commercials made in the development of the model. The effect of advertising seems to be limited to priming particular concerns and to informing voters as to where the candidates stand. Exposure does not seem to change the perception of where the candidates stand on particular issues, nor does it have a significant impact on the positions voters take for themselves. I am not claiming that ads never persuade, over the course of a campaign, many ads on the same subject may move the median-voter's position. However, it seems safe to conclude that only the effects of priming and learning in the form of opinionation need to be taken into account by a model of campaigns.

FORMAL ANALYSIS

In this section, I describe the game, which is a formal model of two-candidate elections. I then use this game to investigate the dynamics

supporting the candidates' choice of themes and the resulting consequences of the candidates' joint behavior for the campaign. Before
detailing the model, I discuss some of the boundaries on the rational
candidate's choices. The game is presented in English, and all of the
mathematical work can be found in appendix A. The chapter concludes
with an analysis of the game that identifies its equilibrium and derives
the proposition that campaign dialogue will never occur if candidates
behave as the model specifies.

The candidates' choices center on message creation, which I reduce
to a decision of how much to discuss each potential theme in the
campaigns. Using polls and the like, candidates and consultants design messages in light of information recovered from the electorate.
This strategic calculus is channeled by the likely effect of the candidates' choices on the electorate's decision. Candidates are forced to use
foresight. Given their accumulated wisdom and using devices like
focus groups, they have a well-grounded expectation concerning how
their messages will alter the voters' cognitive maps, and therefore,
the vote.

Consider the calculus surrounding the subject of public safety. Both
candidates may well know that a majority of the public favors getting
tough on crime. The candidates can reasonably expect that this attitu-
dinal posture will remain constant for the campaign's duration. Therefore, it is unlikely that either candidate will engage in efforts to persuade
the public that getting tough is not the answer. Further, the public probably will perceive one of the candidates, whether due to partisanship,
gender, reputation, or the like, as being closer to the majority's ideal.
The closer-positioned candidate can take advantage of this situation. He
or she will likely advertise on the subject of crime. Extrapolating from
the above discussion of empirical research, the advantaged candidate
expects to inform a portion of the public and to increase the weight
voters accord crime when casting their ballots. Thus, although campaign effects may be limited to increases in opinionation and to priming
particular dimensions, these effects leave ample room for rational candidates to engage in campaign activities.

Finally, candidates have limited budgets. Ads cost money, which
must be raised, usually through the direct action of the candidate
(Alexander 1992; Sorauf 1992). An ad on one issue necessarily displaces
an ad addressing a second consideration. The candidate's time is also
valuable: every second spent exclusively emphasizing a particular theme
means a second lost to any other. With a limited budget and fixed

costs, the candidate's resource allocation task becomes an optimization problem. Because there are two candidates optimizing in a noncooperative way, game-theory is the appropriate tool for formal analysis.

The Game-Theoretic Model

The game takes place in a multidimensional psychological space with many dimensions called public opinion. Each dimension represents a potential campaign theme – any subject that a candidate can discuss which can also affect the vote. This space abstracts the collective mind of the electorate and is characterized by two kinds of values. In the first place, the electorate has a distribution of latent predispositions or preferences associated with each dimension. The electorate also has a chronic level of concern for each dimension. Chronic concern represents the importance the electorate attaches to particular themes in the absence of a campaign (a default value). For example, economic evaluations typically play a large role in presidential approval, but in extreme circumstances, like the Gulf War, the foundations of presidential approval change (Krosnick and Kinder 1990).

There are two candidates, called "D" and "R." Each candidate has positions on each dimension that quickly become known to the electorate. Once known, these positions are immobile. Candidates' positions depend in part on their partisanship. Democrats are generally on the left of issues while their Republican opponents are on the right (Lodge and Hamill 1986; Palfrey and Rosenthal 1985). The positions are also idiosyncratic to the extent that some candidates are more or less liberal or conservative than their copartisans. Campaign budgets, which I assume to be distributed symmetrically, are allocated in the process of message creation. If a candidate decides to spend half of his or her money discussing a particular theme, then half of the overall message will focus on that theme.

The joint set of allocations is the campaign. The campaign can be thought of as a vector of allocations extending across all dimensions. If candidates choose not to spend any money, then that value is zero; otherwise, the value is the proportion of the budget allocated to that dimension by both candidates.

Candidates are only concerned about winning, which I take to mean maximizing the expected vote share. (They may also be said to care about policy because they cannot change their positions to increase their vote share.) Because voter feedback is unreliable, the candidates do not know the exact locations of the median voter's ideal point. However, they do have expectations generated by polls, expert advice, and previous experience. With respect to any theme, voters are more satisfied (their utility increases) as a candidate's stance moves closer to their own preferences. The candidate whose stance is closest to the median-voter will have the advantage on any particular dimension.

Candidates' positions on public safety serve again to illustrate these points. Assuming voters' preferences can be ordered so that those on the left side believe in less punitive measures, the distribution of predispositions concerning public safety can be normalized, placing the median-voter at the scale's center. Candidate D can be expected to favor less punitive measures, like job-training programs. Candidate R, in contrast, would favor more punishment, perhaps in the form of increased spending on prisons. Assume further that D is farther away from the median voter than R in absolute terms. As it stands, if crime is the only issue, R, closer to the median, would win. With more than one issue, voters sum across themes to decide the election.

Play centers on the candidates' budget allocations, which affect the way voters weight considerations when choosing between candidates. The proportion of total campaign spending on a given theme, the effectiveness of advertising at changing the salience of theme, and the slack in public concern relative to voters' chronic level of concern together determine the final weight associated with each theme. Weights change as the salience of considerations in the voters' minds change, and are the target of candidates' attempts to prime the electorate. The more important or salient a dimension becomes relative to other dimensions, the larger its final weight. Every allocation made by either candidate to discussing a particular theme is assumed to increase its weight. However, allocations have diminishing marginal returns, as early spending will likely have a greater impact than later spending.

The game proceeds in the following way. First, the given parameters – the voters' ideal points, initial weights, and the candidates' stances – are randomly drawn from the appropriate distributions. Working within these parameters, candidates design their messages, creating the campaign vector. Then, the campaign takes place. (This version of the game does not allow for campaign dynamics, so the campaign, somewhat artificially, occurs simultaneously and instantaneously.) Voters make their choices, deciding which candidate's election will yield the greatest benefit. The election ends, one candidate wins, and the winning candidate implements the given positions and policies.

Issue Selection and Dialogue

Two questions arise from this framework. What themes should the candidates choose to discuss? And, how should they allocate their budgets? Given the construction of the model, the candidates' allocation strategies depend exclusively on the relative positions of the candidates. Consistent with the priming effect, the allocations have a direct influence on the weights voters use to calculate their satisfaction; thus, the importance of a consideration in calculating the vote increases monotonically with campaign expenditures. Following Black's (1958) logic, a candidate does best in terms of increasing expected vote by choosing those themes on which he or she is relatively closer to the median-voter's expected position. The number of themes each candidate chooses is determined by the marginal return to spending on each theme and the number of advantageous themes available. For instance, if there are decreasing marginal returns to spending (in terms of increasing salience), then at some point the candidate will switch to discussing the second most advantageous theme.

Returning to the priming example illustrates the intuition that candidates will campaign on issues where they are already closer to the median voter. Given the candidates' positions, the relative positioning of candidates determines where campaign resources are best allocated. The priming figure, Figure 4.1, underscores this point. D is advantaged by his or her relative closeness to the voter's expected ideal point on dimension y; D expects to receive more votes as the weight on dimension y increases. In contrast, if the election turns on dimension x, D will lose. Thus, in this two-dimensional example, D should (and presumably will) spend only on dimension y.

Candidates want to win and try to do so by emphasizing certain themes over others in their campaign message. Their joint choices – the campaign – affect the weight voters attach to discussed themes. The critical connection is that the weight accorded to a dimension can only increase as candidates devote resources toward that dimension.

If the candidates differ on any theme, given the ideal point of the median-voter, only one candidate has the advantage. (The special case where candidates are equidistant from the median voter is discussed in chapter seven.) Because voters' weights monotonically increase with respect to budget allocations, the advantage of the closer candidate increases as he or she allocates resources toward discussing that theme. In fact, the advantage of the closer candidate also increases should the candidate who is further away allocate any resources to that theme.

Thus, even with decreasing marginal returns to campaign spending, the candidates would spend infinite amounts of money on the themes where they are advantaged (notwithstanding the budget constraint) and none on themes where they are disadvantaged.

Imagine a case with two issues, the economy and social issues. Recall that the candidates know where they stand in relation to the median voter on these dimensions. Assume that one candidate is advantaged due to a better position on the economy. That candidate will only talk about the economy. Economic statistics, plans, and programs will consume the overwhelming share of that candidate's resources. The candidate's goal is to inform the public that his or her position is indeed better, while raising the salience of the economy as an issue.

The opponent has a choice between defending a losing position on the economy or shifting to social issues. From the rational perspective outlined above, the opponent's choice is equally clear. None of the opponent's money will be spent talking about the economy; rather, all resources will go toward the discussion of social issues. Again, the opponent's goal is to inform the public of the relative positions on social issues and to increase the importance of this consideration in determining the electorate's decision. The outcome of these individual choices is that there will be no dialogue. The entire campaign will be characterized by an absence of dialogue.

In sum, rational candidates should, and will, spend their entire budget on dimensions that work to increase their advantage by informing voters of their positions and priming that consideration. As no themes can work to the advantage of both candidates, they will never allocate resources to the same theme. Dialogue is defined as candidates discussing (spending money on) the same dimension, so, rational candidates should never and will never dialogue.

Conclusion

Working backward from an empirical understanding of campaign effects, my analysis (to this point) utterly proscribes dialogue in campaign discourse. However, there is dialogue of some kind in almost every election, so this blanket statement is admittedly questionable. To preview later refinements, dialogue arises under conditions assumed away by the previous analysis. When candidates lie or one candidate has an overwhelming amount of money, the likelihood of dialogue increases. Similarly, when the campaign's arena (public opinion) is effectively limited to one issue, there will also be dialogue. Finally, there are special circumstances when the model anticipates dialogue. When candidates' positions are arrayed so that discussing a given theme equally advantages them, dialogue is more likely to occur. When voters are especially susceptible to direct persuasion effects or otherwise immune to candidate priming, dialogue is likely to increase.

Before discussing these points in detail, I present a case study in chapter five. It examines an election where one candidate attempted to win an election via the creation of a meaningful dialogue and failed. Using the experimental dataset previewed in this chapter, I confirm the empirical prediction concerning dialogue's ineffectiveness as a vote-getting strategy.

CHAPTER 5

Duck or Punch? Dialogue in a California Gubernatorial Election

The 1994 California gubernatorial race presents an ideal situation to study the dynamics of campaign strategy with respect to the question of dialogue. It is also a classic piece of political drama. Kathleen Brown, the Democratic challenger, was by all accounts destined to win. Blessed with a national following as a rising star in the Democratic party, she attracted extraordinary early funding, had weak opposition within the party, and had established a solid reputation as state treasurer. Early polls (see Table 5.6, for details) showed Brown leading by a twenty-point margin. Pete Wilson, her Republican opponent, appeared to be a doomed incumbent, burdened by a statewide economic recession and a contentious Democrat-controlled state legislature. A year before the election, a *Los Angeles Times* poll placed Wilson's approval rating at a dismal 29 percent. Yet, on election day, Wilson won a decisive fourteen-point victory, recast himself as a powerful figure in the national Republican party, and left Brown's political reputation in ruins. Why? I argue that this defeat was largely the result of Brown's decision to dialogue on the subject of crime. Thus, this case study serves as an empirical demonstration of the dangers of dialogue and provides a cautionary tale to those who would expect dialogue in any strong form from contemporary campaigns.

This election exemplifies a clash between two different approaches to campaigning. It pitted Brown's more traditional campaign style against Wilson's more contemporary approach, an approach consistent with what I consider to be a modern campaign. Brown was dedicated to creating dialogue while the Wilson candidacy was dedicated, by its own admission, to shaping an agenda favorable to Pete Wilson's electoral returns. His campaign team focused its efforts on priming the electorate to think about crime and immigration, issues where Wilson's position

66

closely matched that of the median voter. On the other hand, the Brown team attempted to persuade the electorate that her crime-related stances were reasonable, either attempting to bring the electorate to her view or to convince them that she was tougher than she appeared. Therefore, Wilson was able to create an environment for the campaign that the Brown team fought within.

Although many factors typically play a role in electoral outcomes, this race was a testament to the skill of Wilson's team, particularly the effectiveness of its strategic choices. Notwithstanding the conclusion drawn by Brown's campaign director, who remarked, "unfortunately for us, the defeat was so decisive and so total that it is very difficult for us to point to that fork in the road when the campaign went south on us" (Lubenow 1995, p. 24). I argue that Wilson's victory was neither pre-destined, nor the result of a simple miscalculation or bad execution on the part of Brown's team. It came from a basic misunderstanding of the dynamic of contemporary campaign discourse. Wilson's operatives were skillful, and their success stemmed from their adoption of a particular campaign strategy. The outcome was thus the result of the dominance of Wilson's strategic paradigm.

My examination of this election provides an empirical test of the no dialogue hypothesis; namely, that a campaign strategy predicated on creating a dialogue will win fewer votes than one based on ignoring an opponent's initiatives. A set of controlled experiments, conducted during the campaign, constitutes the main portion of this case study. These experiments followed a highly naturalistic procedure that featured likely voters who viewed and responded to a sample of commercials actually employed by the candidates (see Ansolabehere and Iyengar 1995; Iyengar and Kinder 1987, for details). Two of the experiments followed a two-ad design. This technique enables the assessment of the strategies the candidates employed, as well as alternative strategies that they chose not to use. These counterfactual conditions were based on ads that the candidates produced but used either sparingly or not at all. One experiment, already covered in the previous chapter, simply assessed the effects of a single Wilson ad in order to test and demonstrate some of the assumptions made about advertising effects. Finally, to corroborate my experimental evidence, I offer sample survey data obtained from a series of statewide polls conducted during the campaign.

WHY STUDY THIS RACE?

The race for governor of California "is exceeded only by a presidential campaign in terms of the pressures and demands it imposes on participants" (Lubenow 1995, p. ix). As the most important election in the largest state, party leaders and political consultants pay close attention. California often sets the agenda for elections nationwide and is a testing ground for new techniques. In part, this is because California elections are much more comparable to presidential elections than most state elections. The sheer size of the state makes the electorate and the candidates heavily dependent on the mass media. The partisan ties of California's voters tend to be weaker than the ties in other states, and there is a relatively high proportion of independents. Much of the electorate has emigrated from elsewhere, leaving its voters without a stable context or strong social bonds to constrain their voting preferences. The proportion of "persuadables," voters whose decision could change in response to the campaign, is relatively high. As the larger society and other political entities come to resemble California more closely in these respects, the lessons of California's campaigns will be that much more valuable.

Just as there are trends in clothes and automobiles, there are trends in political campaigning. Consultants and campaign managers are quick to copy successful innovations, and Wilson's dramatic victory proved to be no exception. The mobility of professional campaign staff hastens the diffusion of campaign technology. Several participants in the Wilson campaign worked for Bob Dole's unsuccessful 1996 presidential campaign, for instance. These participants and other observers undoubtedly will try again, attempting to use the tools that proved successful in California on other races.

More important, this race provides a unique opportunity to study the consequences of dialogue. The two candidates came down squarely on opposite sides of the question of dialogue's vote-getting value. Given the Darwinian, survival of the fittest nature of politics – that is, the imitation of successful techniques and the abandonment of unsuccessful ones – this kind of head-to-head clash of opposing campaign philosophies is rare, and therefore a valuable opportunity for study. To push the analogy further, imagine two species competing for the same ecological niche in the aftermath of a severe climatic change. Over the long term, the better-adapted species would thrive, leaving its less well-adapted cousins extinct. However, for a brief period, the species would coexist, albeit in competition. This gubernatorial race represented such a clash of opposing schools. Further, Wilson's dim prospects before the campaign, followed by his victory, alert us as well as other candidates to the effectiveness of his technique, and the penalties associated with Brown's adoption of dialogue as a campaign strategy.

My task is to link the outcome of this election directly to the strategy of the candidates, and to the particular messages that these strategies produced. To show that a candidate used a particular strategy and then won would leave my contentions open to several objections, as he or she could have won for any number of reasons. It is necessary to demonstrate that the candidates' behavior in the form of their strategic choices determined this outcome. Fortunately, this race has an extraordinary array of data available for the pursuit of empirical study. Among the unusual sources of information is a publication by the Institute for Governmental Studies (IGS) at the University of California at Berkeley, detailing the mindset and intentions of the campaigners. The IGS conference attracted a set of political professionals who participated in an essentially open hearing on their campaign experiences. Social scientists, public pollsters, and members of the press who were versed in the idiosyncrasies of this race also attended. The presence of members of the opposing candidates' teams, as well as more or less impartial political communication experts created a dialogue about the rationale behind and the effects of campaign activity.

Access to such information is ordinarily stymied by the fact that candidates do not want to be seen as strategic. Sincerity equates to political virtue, while the rational calculation it takes to win an election is taken for unseemly scheming. Further complicating the search for truth is the professional self-interest of political operatives who naturally wish to appear omniscient and, therefore, omnipotent. In the aftermath of a campaign, all losses are predestined, mistakes are rationalized, and victories are linked to generic and even genetic political skill. Students of campaigns are often forced to rely on their own intuitions, or on journalists' accounts of the campaign, to discern the strategic intentions. At best, one may be able to conduct interviews of the participants, assuming they grant access and are reasonably forthcoming. In contrast to this murky picture, this conference produced a volume that goes some way toward providing the requisite inside information. So, while some of their statements may be self-serving rationalizations, at least they come straight from the participants immediately after the campaign in an open hearing. It is largely from this account that I reconstruct the candidates' strategic calculations.

BACKGROUND

This gubernatorial election, despite its peculiar features, fits the general model of elections and campaigns developed in chapter four. Each candidate had a set of self-perceived strengths and weaknesses and designed a campaign strategy in the face of these, the opponent's strengths and weaknesses, and the electorate's predispositions. The predispositions were in part the result of exogenous factors, or external events, that neither candidate controlled, but that influenced the outcome. I will briefly run through all the exogenous factors that formed the political environment, both to illustrate them and to show how the model applies to a particular situation. I then focus on the strategic calculations that ensued given the relative stances of the candidates and the median-voter. My purpose here is to underscore the difference in campaign approaches with respect to the question of message construction. Specifically, I trace the strategizing on behalf of both Brown and Wilson that led to dialogue on the subject of crime in the actual campaign.

The period prior to the election was difficult for California. That the events of this period seemed to have worked to Wilson's advantage is somewhat paradoxical, given that economic malaise usually curtails an incumbent's advantage. Aside from the economy, there were three big news stories, the aftermath of the civil unrest in Los Angeles following the Rodney King verdict, the Northridge earthquake of January 17, 1994, and the O. J. Simpson trial. Immediately prior to the campaign another tragedy occurred when Polly Klaas, a twelve-year-old girl from Petaluma, California, was murdered. This crime and the public outrage following it undoubtedly furthered Wilson's goal. By 1994, the "year of the woman," which saw an increase in the number of female office-holders, was over. In its place was a rising Republican tide that led to their capture of the House and Senate for the first time in many decades. Of course, not all of California's women Democrats lost. Dianne Feinstein, for example, held on to her newly won Senate seat. As far as the Republican tide is concerned, Paul Holm, a Republican pollster not connected to the Wilson campaign, estimated that it added "three or four points to Pete Wilson's final numbers" (Lubenow 1995, p. 124).

Campaign finance is another important factor to rule out. As has been said, money is the mother's milk of politics, and Brown and

Wilson's reliance on money in this contest was typical. Only dollars could have bought the ads Wilson and Brown used to send their messages. Without ads, the candidates would have lost their voices and been written off by the media and the candidate and the campaign would have disappeared. However, my model assumes candidates have equal access to communicative resources and, thus, finance is irrelevant to dialogue. Was this true in the California race? Within reason it was true in its early and middle phases. Wilson ended up outspending Brown in the general election almost 2 to 1, approximately $20 million to $12 million. Yet, this disparity was arguably the result of Brown's strategic failure. Prior to the end of the race, neither candidate lacked money. In fact, the volume of money the candidates were able to raise and spend impressed pundits. Brown did "go dark" during the final week of the campaign. She ran out of money because, "major Democratic contributors smelled a loss and just shut their wallets," according to Dan Borenstein, a Brown staffer (Lubenow 1995, p. 50). However, it is too simplistic to blame this fact for her loss because she had sufficient access to funds during the campaign's critical period.

The potential contributors' second thoughts were due to poll results showing Brown far behind ten days before the election. The poll results were themselves the result of campaign decisions. Brown had already spent over $12 million at that point (not counting primary spending), and had already substantially disseminated her message. One might guess that a tighter race would have produced more money for Brown and less for Wilson in the last stages of the campaign, dramatically changing the spending ratio. While money is undoubtedly important, in itself it neither caused nor would have changed the outcome.

THE ISSUES

My model relies heavily on a representation of public opinion as a multidimensional space. It is critical to understand how the architects of the respective candidate's strategy understood the political environment facing them. In other words, what themes did the candidates consider in the process of message creation? According to Celinda Lake, Brown's pollster and strategist: "There were three issues out there: immigration, crime, and the economy." From the Republican side, George Gorton, a Wilson strategist, reinforces this view: "Reporters seem to think there were only two issues, crime and immigration. We worried every single day about the economy." To these three, Brown herself added education. She felt it necessary to give major speeches on

71

only these three issues and on education. These constituted her positions for the press (and presumably for Wilson) in the fall prior to 1994.
Education is also appropriate to consider in this discussion because of
the role it played in both candidates' campaign planning, as well as the
role it could have played in the campaign. These four areas – crime, the
economy, immigration, and education – were considered by both candidates in their strategic calculations and made up the overwhelming
share of the content of the campaign.

CRIME. From the beginning, everyone expected public safety would
play a major role in the campaign. Wilson and his team loved his
reputation for being tough on crime. The candidates' stances and reputations on crime-related issues could not have suited Wilson better.
Unlike many Democrats, such as Dianne Feinstein, Brown had taken a
firm anti–death penalty stance. Wilson, in contrast, appeared eager to
enforce the death penalty. He matched this enthusiasm with support for
the three-strikes initiative which mandated twenty-five-years-to-life
sentences for criminals found guilty of a third felony and, later, a
"one strike" policy imposing mandatory sentences on those convicted
of rape. Wilson also garnered the endorsement of almost every leading
law enforcement association. Brown, on the other hand, had the
endorsement of just one police union.

THE ECONOMY. Whether in terms of job creation, inflation, or something else, the state of the economy is a perennial campaign theme.
Brown's reputation as treasurer and California's dismal economic performance during Wilson's term gave the Brown team reason to believe
that they held the upper hand as far as the economy was concerned.
According to Clint Reilly, head of the Brown campaign, "You guys can
take the position that I'm a dunce or an idiot. But we believed at that
stage of the campaign that the economy would be a winning issue for
the Democratic candidate." This view led Brown and her campaign staff
to devise the slogan, "Restore the promise for middle-class families," in
July of 1994. By October, this theme evolved into the, "Plan for Building a New California" (Lubenow 1995, p. 50). This plan was a modest
set of government-related economic policy proposals, centered around
cutting state government by $5 billion and investing that money in cre-
ating jobs, education, and making the streets safer. As far as economic
matters were concerned, Wilson focused his rhetoric on the number of
jobs created during his administration, but as George Gorton indicated,
the notion of the economy as an important campaign consideration
filled Wilson's staff with discomfort.

IMMIGRATION. The shape of the immigration issue was determined by a ballot initiative with which Wilson was closely associated, though not officially linked. Proposition 187 essentially called for limiting or eliminating illegal immigrants' access to government services. Public support for Proposition 187 was very high until October, when it dropped to only majority support. Support for the measure did not fall further after this point in time. Wilson's slogan, "There is a right way and a wrong way, and to reward the wrong way is not the American way," matched the median-voter's position almost perfectly. His pleas for federal government assistance in dealing with immigration-related costs also garnered a great deal of public approval. Brown, in contrast, was ideologically opposed to Proposition 187. Her sentiments were strongly reinforced by the presence of Latino groups in her presumptive coalition. Consequently, Brown found herself closely allied with the only significant bloc of opposition to this measure, in the face of solid majority support.

EDUCATION. As a dimension impinging on the election, education was more of an also-ran. However, this does not mean that the candidates did not consider this subject when formulating their strategies. It also does not mean that education could not have been an important consideration under alternative strategies. On the face of it, Brown appeared to be better positioned on education. George Gorton remarked:

> Education was something we were always very concerned about. We thought we would have to spend a certain period of time on education, and it would be a difficult argument for us to make. You have the CTA (California Teachers' Association), you have a woman liberal Democrat, and certainly the schools need a lot of help. So we assumed education would be one of the big three issues. And that worried us a lot (Lubenow 1995, p. 89).

The chronic problems with California's public schools, the support of the teachers, and her natural credibility seemed to make this theme tailor-made for Brown. Wilson's only serious link to this dimension was negative; he had proposed rather severe cuts in state educational support because of budgetary problems. However, as detailed below, Brown's strategy led to the disappearance of education as an issue. Her strategic decision in this area illustrates well the difference in campaign philosophies between her and Wilson.

THE STRATEGIES

Against this backdrop Wilson's strategic calculus proceeded smoothly, and was summed up best by Dick Dresner, his pollster. Using the standard techniques of the modern campaign, polls and focus groups, Wilson's strategists discovered that people would say, "Yeah, I don't like Pete Wilson," and when asked why, they'd say, "Well, he hasn't done anything that I've heard about, so he mustn't be doing a good job." Dresner claims that they "discovered there was really no personal animosity between voters and Pete Wilson. There was a tremendous opportunity to fill in the blanks" (Lubenow 1995, p. 121). As a consequence, again according to Dresner, the Wilson campaign,

> set out to occupy three issue spaces, and we took them one at a time. The first was crime. By making that an issue, by emphasizing the differences between Wilson and Brown, we gained a lot of ground . . . The next one was immigration, and we went out to a tremendous lead on that. But the third one we always felt was the economy. You cannot run in this state and ignore what is happening with the economy. We were fortunate that people never really blamed it on Pete Wilson (Lubenow 1995, p. 143).

Thus, Wilson's message centered on three issues: crime, immigration, and the economy, roughly in that order. Crime and, to a lesser extent, immigration commanded the greatest share of his resources.

The Brown campaign, in contrast, seemed to have difficulty articulating a single strategy. We can, however, reconstruct the calculations that led to choosing some campaign messages over others. According to Reilly, the Brown team initially considered three lines of attack. In the first place, Brown considered attacking Wilson's job performance and putting Brown forward as a leader who could "put the state back on track," entailing a strategic focus on the economy and on education. The campaign managers apparently feared this approach would not work. Reilly claimed that their research, presumably focus groups and polls, indicated that a more promising avenue was a populist message targeted at middle-class voters, again prescribing a focus on the economy. Reilly seemed to believe that Brown's stances, especially on the death penalty, were not ideologically consistent with a campaign focus on the economy; thus Reilly (apparently at odds with other Brown staff) decided that an attack on crime was necessary to ameliorate the negative impact of her anti–death penalty view. The third strategy he alluded to was an attack on Wilson, presumably on the subject of crime or immigration (Lubenow 1995, p. 72).

Shortly after the primary the Brown team appeared to adopt the third strategy; the Brown campaign actually attacked Wilson's stance on crime, giving less attention to the economy and almost none to education. Reilly recounts Brown's objective this way: "We were trying to deal with the issue of crime to the extent that we could build some credibility and neutralize Kathleen's position on the death penalty" (Lubenow 1995, p. 76). In an attempt to inoculate against weakness, Kathleen Brown made crime the subject of her first serious initiative of the campaign. Tactically, Brown's crime message was two-pronged. The first prong was an attempt to attack Wilson's poor performance in dealing with the problem of crime and the need to take steps that were more effective. For example, in a seeming attempt to recapture the "Willie Horton Effect," Brown attacked Wilson for releasing an inmate named Melvin Carter. The second prong evolved later in the campaign; it revolved around attempting to merge the issues of crime and education. Brown's message featured ads focusing on juvenile felons and the importance of school safety.

Brown at least initially avoided education and seemed to avoid emphasis on the economy in favor of talking about crime. Michael Reese, Brown's deputy campaign manager, stated "the strategy pre-Clint and post-Clint [Reilly] was that we had to neutralize crime and immigration as best we could." He concluded, "that was a process we tried to do throughout, but, from the beginning, we knew we were not going to win either of those two issues" (Lubenow 1995, p. 87). To this comment, Don Sipple, who worked for Wilson, responded, "We would disagree whether the issue was Melvin Carter or one strike. Whatever the specifics, you're arguing within the context of our strongest issue" (Lubenow 1995, p. 85).

Why was education dealt with in this way? After some urging on the part of her colleagues at the IGS conference, Celinda Lake, Brown's pollster and strategist, discussed the Brown campaign's attitudes on other issues, notably education. "The problem was that it (education) was clearly a fourth-tier issue for everyone else, and we were doing fairly well in Northern California with the education voters. By the general (election) we were spread thin on money, so we were pulling our ads out of Northern California, out of the female market, into Southern California, into men. Yes, it was a good issue for us, but we felt we had that issue." The response to this logic by George Gorton highlights the differences, "That's not our theory of politics. We would have pounded education, to move it into a first-tier issue, make it the issue people walk into the ballot box thinking about. If they walk into the ballot box thinking about education, it's going to be very difficult for a conservative Republican man to win." Dick Dresner reiterates this sentiment and provides a succinct statement of the Wilson team's method, and perhaps the best overall summary of the contemporary campaigner's goals:

> The thing that sort of surprised me was the education issue. Our concept of how to approach the issue is not to ask if 10 people are concerned about the issue can I go from seven of those people to eight, and increase my vote? The more important question is, can I expand the number interested in an issue? If I can control the agenda and expand the number of people who are concerned about immigration or crime, then I can change their focus from something else, whether it's the environment or education or whatever (Lubenow 1995, p. 79).

Conclusion: Wilson's Victory; Dialogue's Failure

Wilson's emphasis on crime and immigration paired with Brown's strategy, which also centered on crime, was accompanied by steadily decreasing poll margins for Brown, ending in a near landslide (see Table 5.6). Wilson's strategists were happy to take credit. Dick Dresner claimed that,

> They were voting for Pete Wilson because of where he stood on an issue. By the end of the campaign in our polls, Pete Wilson was a popular governor. It was no longer a question of "Who is this guy and what has he done?" If you asked people what the governor had done at the end (which we did in focus groups) they knew about three strikes, they knew about one strike, they knew about immigration and they even knew about some of the things he'd done in terms of the economy (Lubenow 1995, p. 123).

Less partisan observers were also quick to credit Wilson's team. John Brennan, pollster for the *Los Angeles Times*, underscored Dresner's point that "illegal immigrants along with violent felons became the focus. It was a master stroke for someone in political trouble" (Lubenow 1995, p. 111). Another public opinion expert, Mark DiCamillo, of the California Poll, agreed. "Asked to volunteer what they liked and disliked about each of the candidates in their own words, voters could easily play back Wilson's two major campaign themes: he's going to be tough on crime, and he's going to be tough on illegal immigration" (Lubenow 1995, p. 119).

Finally, even members of Wilson's opposition agreed that the key to his victory lay in the campaign. Paul Maslin, Democratic pollster:

> One lesson we should all learn from the gubernatorial campaign is that these things don't come from thin air. That's not the way this process works. Dick summed it up when he said it's not a passive process. He's absolutely right. It was an active process by a campaign that said, "We don't like this situation and we're going to change it." And they did it as well as any campaign I've ever seen in my life. Like it or not, they executed extraordinarily well (Lubenow 1995, p. 127).

In sum, the Wilson campaign managed to capitalize on his reputation, external events and the public's predispositions while Brown's efforts probably only served to increase attention to issue dimensions favorable to Wilson, winning her few votes. By choosing to engage in dialogue on a theme of Wilson's choosing, the Brown campaign squandered her early lead, curtailed her ability to raise funds, and gave the appearance of political incompetence. From a theoretical standpoint, these electoral results strongly support the model's prediction.

The "what if" question, raised by Michael Reese during the course of the conference, is the point of departure for the next section of empirical study. "What if she had seized education as an issue with the same vigor that Wilson had seized immigration? What if 'The Plan' had been released earlier and with the financial resources needed to make an impact" (Lubenow 1995, p. 63)? In other words, what if Brown abandoned dialogue and followed the same generic strategy as Wilson? It is to this question that the next section turns.

RATIONALE FOR STUDY DESIGN

Experimental designs provide a rigorous test of causality. The logic is simple; the researcher compares the effects of two messages or sets of messages while eliminating all confounding factors. In this case, the design tests whether it was the candidates' strategic choices (in the form of combinations of advertisements) that caused the change in voting intentions. An exhaustive account of the experimental setting, participants, and procedures is supplied in appendix B.

It is often difficult to establish the causal role of campaign communications. For example, if a challenger advertises a plan for economic recovery and defeats the incumbent, at least three interpretations are available. First, the proponent of campaign effects holds that the message was the cause and that had the message changed, so too would have the election's outcome. Second, some relatively objective circumstance, in this illustration the actual state of the economy, may have caused the defeat and the message itself was incidental. If so, the relationship between message and outcome is spurious. Finally, the causal order may be reversed. The challenger may have chosen to focus advertisements on the subject of the economy, because voters were already concerned with that issue. Experimental techniques are a convenient and powerful way to disentangle these options and isolate the proper explanation.

The experimental method also enables the investigation of counterfactual phenomena. In the real world, only one course of campaign events can be observed. Experiments allow the researcher to simulate a series of strategic choices on behalf of each candidate. As a whole, the experimental design devised here allowed each potential candidate's message to be paired with each of the opponent's potential messages. Of course, the brief exposure to campaign ads mandated by the experimental setting is not of the same order of magnitude of exposure in an actual campaign. Nevertheless, these experimental results suggest which strategy would have been optimal, in terms of maximizing favorable vote intentions, for each candidate.

The experiments were administered from September 4 to November 2 of the 1994 California gubernatorial race. (Appendix B presents a complete description of the procedure.) As in Shanto Iyengar's work, the study employs a naturalistic approach designed to approximate a home environment, increasing confidence in the validity of the findings (Ansolabehere and Iyengar 1995; Iyengar and Kinder 1987). All of the data reported comes from adult subjects. Many other steps were taken to increase validity. The stimuli were real television ads, and the subjects were purposefully misled as to the true purpose of the experiment in order to avoid demand characteristics or cueing participants to give answers desired by the experimenter (Campbell and Stanley 1967).

Given the campaign's history, there are two specific predictions about the effect of Brown's and Wilson's advertising. The first prediction concerns the best response to make in light of an opponent's choice. This is a direct test of the dialogue hypothesis. Dialogue is operationalized as follows: When faced with an opponent's choice of a dimension, candidates can either acquiesce in the opponent's choice of topic or they can try to change the subject by picking a different dimension. Dialogue only occurs when candidates do not change the subject.

The second prediction concerns the optimal choice of themes by a single candidate. In line with the claims made in the previous chapter, the model predicts that the candidate will gain the most votes by emphasizing dimensions on which he or she is closest to the median voter. Empirically, this suggests that the candidates will do better structuring their message around their best themes rather than spending time discussing themes on which the opponent's position is closer to that of the median voter. In other words, candidates should avoid attempts to inoculate against weakness. Inoculation is operationalized as follows: When constructing their campaign message, candidates can inoculate by attempting to preempt on dimensions thought to be favorable to an opponent; alternatively, they can stick to advertising on just those dimensions most likely to be favorable to them. A successful strategy based on inoculation would lead to dialogue, thus disconfirming the model.

Dialogue has thus far been the subject of scholarly and popular discussion, but not of extensive empirical scrutiny. Changing the subject seems to be a dominant strategy according to conventional wisdom (Petrocik 1996; Budge and Farlie 1983). Petrocik's (1996) "issue ownership" view is particularly interesting in this regard. He posits that there is a well-understood difference between the two major parties' perceived competence on each issue dimension. Republicans, for example, are generally thought to be better at conducting foreign policy. Therefore, Democratic pretensions to foreign policy expertise will not be credible. The electorate chooses the party whose competencies best match the situation. The candidate achieves more by stressing the most relevant dimension on which he or she has an advantage in perceived competency, and never discussing an area when he or she is not perceived to be competent. This view, and its associated evidence, support the preliminary prediction that the candidate should only talk about his or her "own" issues.

On the other hand, many political consultants argue that the candidate should respond in kind to rivals' initiatives. While this dictum is most closely associated with personal attacks, the logic behind it extends to every campaign theme. Using the "marketplace of ideas" logic, it would seem that letting an opponent's initiative go unchallenged grants it legitimacy in the eyes of the voting audience. As Roger Ailes has been quoted as saying, "punch back when punched" (quoted in Ansolabehere, Behr, and Iyengar 1993). Adherents of this school would favor the dialogue strategy.

Inoculation attempts spring from the same logic. Given an array of stances on many issues, political agents can determine which are the most popular for a candidate and, therefore, the most likely to be employed. The opposing candidate, in this event, can anticipate a likely message and prepare a response forewarning the electorate of up-coming content. Candidates can also attempt to inoculate themselves against weakness. For instance, knowing that he or she is faced with a scandalous charge, a candidate may attempt to broadcast rebuttal messages, even in the absence of an opponent's attacks. In the California race, Brown's relatively unpopular opposition to the death penalty was perceived as a weakness and the subject of inoculation attempts.

In sum, my model predicts that candidates will never end up discussing the same issue dimension; thus, the campaign will contain no dialogue. From the perspective of the choosing candidate, any dialogue-enhancing strategy is dominated or suboptimal in terms of votes. The experimental prediction is clear – dialogue and inoculation should generate fewer votes relative to their dialogue-diminishing substitutes.

DIALOGUE EXPERIMENT

A pair of two-ad experiments assesses the main questions raised by the model and the California race. The first experiment assesses the effectiveness of dialogue as a campaign strategy. Is a candidate better off discussing the same subject as the opponent (enhancing dialogue) or ignoring an opponent's initiative by responding with a message on a different subject? Of course, the model predicts the latter strategy will garner more votes. The two-ad design exposed participants to two political commercials. One was inserted in the first break and another was inserted into the second break of a twelve-minute selection taken from a local news broadcast. Table 5.1 presents a list of all combinations used in the design.

This methodology provides an opportunity to test for strategic effects by allowing the assessment of particular combinations of advertisements. In the illustration (Figure 5.1), two conditions are portrayed. In each condition, Wilson advertises on the theme of crime. Brown's

Table 5.1   *Dialogue Experiment: Strategic Combinations and Results*

Condition	First Ad	Second Ad	Mean Vote	N of Subjects
Dialogue	Wilson crime	Brown crime	−.13	39
Ignore	Wilson crime	Brown economy	.0	36
Ignore	Wilson crime	Brown education	.02	52
Dialogue	Brown economy	Wilson economy	.26	19
Ignore	Brown economy	Wilson crime	.05	20
Ignore	Brown economy	Wilson immigration	−.05	18
Dialogue	Brown education	Wilson education	.09	22
Ignore	Brown education	Wilson crime	−.13	23
Ignore	Brown education	Wilson immigration	.09	23

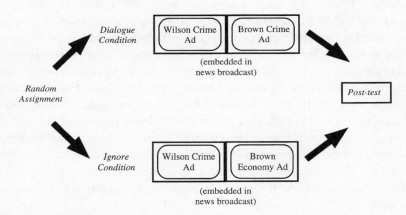

Figure 5.1   Dialogue experiment: Sample of two-ad design.

response then determines whether dialogue will occur. In the dialogue condition, she responds to Wilson's ad with her own ad on crime; while in the ignore condition, she broadcasts an ad on the economy.

Other issue dimensions are used to replicate the basic comparison between dialogue approach and a strategy of simply ignoring the opponent. Again, Table 5.1 lists all the themes employed. Wilson is presumed to lead with his best issue, crime, while Brown is presumed to lead with her best themes, the economy and education. The response determines the condition. In the dialogue conditions, the opponent responds on the same issue dimension as the first advertisement. Wilson's ad on crime is answered by one from Brown. In the ignore conditions, the better of the candidate's issues takes the place of a dialogue response. Wilson's ad on crime is answered by Brown's ad on the economy or education.

In the parlance of experimental science, this design has three factors, each having two levels. The first factor corresponds to the initiating candidate, in this case, Brown or Wilson. The second factor corresponds to the theme that the initiating candidate advertised – the economy or education for Brown and crime or immigration for Wilson. The third factor represents the opposing candidate's response – ignore or dialogue. The design is not fully orthogonal because Brown never produced an ad on immigration, eliminating three of the twelve possible conditions.

The experiment's central result concerns the effect of the strategic pairings on the aggregate vote. This data is presented in the right-hand column of Table 5.1. Brown does best when she shows an ad on the economy and Wilson creates dialogue with her by also presenting an ad on the economy. Among these participants, Brown wins by 26 percent. Wilson does best in two conditions – when Brown attempts to dialogue on crime and when Wilson ignores Brown's initiative on education and responds with an ad on crime. Among these two sets of participants, Wilson wins by 13 percentage points. The crime dialogue condition closely resembles how the actual race proceeded at the outset. It is interesting to note that Brown garnered more support when her ads ignored Wilson's crime message and dealt with alternative issues, such as her views on the economy or on education. These responses produced a virtual dead heat. I will return to a more general assessment of this point below.

Table 5.2 presents the overall results. The appropriate comparison is between the conditions representing a candidate's choice to dialogue and the conditions where the candidate makes the best possible response. Constructing the comparison in this way enables us to assess the opportunity cost of dialogue. What happens when a candidate chooses to devote thirty seconds of airtime to dialogue as opposed to spending that unit of airtime in a way that will garner votes most effectively? Again, a regression model specification assessed the effect of this choice after controlling for the effects of partisan identification. In this estimation, the data have been recoded so that positive numbers favor the candidate who made the choice. On average, the choice to dialogue costs the candidate 21 percentage points or one-fifth of the electorate. In comparison, the subject's partisanship accounts for roughly three-

Table 5.2   *Dialogue Experiment: Strategies' Overall Effect on Vote*

Dialogue	−.21**
	(.10)
Subject's party	.57**
	(.06)
(Constant)	.14
N	156
Adj. R-square	38%

Note: Entries are OLS regression coefficients with standard errors in parentheses. Dialogue dummy scored zero = absence of dialogue, one = dialogue present. Asterisks represent approximate significance levels: ** = p < .05.

fifths of the subject's vote. The penalty associated with dialogue is large and statistically significant even after controlling for partisan effects.

INOCULATION EXPERIMENT

The second experiment concerns message construction by a single candidate. Do candidates do better when structuring messages around themes that favor them, or will an inoculation strategy prove more effective? Inoculation involves preempting an opponent's best potential themes via advertising. Should candidates stick to their own message, concentrating on themes they "own," or should their advertisements feature themes their opponents might use? In this way inoculation is like dialogue, given the assumption that the opposing candidates will opt to discuss themes favorable to themselves. The main difference between inoculation and dialogue is that inoculation treats the actions of a single candidate as opposed to a pair of candidates. The theoretical prediction is that inoculation, like dialogue, will be a less than optimal strategy.

Eight pairs of issues were used. Half were in each of the conditions. The choice to inoculate was operationalized by replacing an ad on a seemingly favorable theme with an ad from the same candidate on a less favorable theme. If the candidate chose not to inoculate, two different ads on the same theme were shown. For instance, two different Brown ads on the economy were compared to one Brown ad on the

Table 5.3   *Inoculation Experiment: Strategic Combinations and Results*

Condition	First Ad	Second Ad	Mean Vote	N of Subjects
Don't Inoculate	Brown education	Brown education	.14	22
Inoculate	Brown education	Brown crime	.0	17
Don't Inoculate	Brown economy	Brown economy	.36	22
Inoculate	Brown economy	Brown crime	.09	23
Don't Inoculate	Wilson crime	Wilson crime	.0	36
Inoculate	Wilson crime	Wilson economy	.14	37
Don't Inoculate	Wilson immigration	Wilson immigration	−.05	21
Inoculate	Wilson immigration	Wilson economy	.0	20

economy and one Brown ad on crime. This experiment follows a 2 × 2 × 2 design, presented in Table 5.3, where the first factor corresponds to the candidate, the second factor corresponds to the candidate's own theme, and the third factor corresponds to the choice of the candidate's second theme, on-message or off-message. If candidates stay on-message, they stick with their best theme; otherwise they go off-message in an attempt to inoculate.

The results also appear in Table 5.3. Brown does best when she shows two ads on the economy – a thirty-six-point lead – while Wilson does best with two ads on immigration giving him a 5 percent lead. Brown also does well – a fourteen-point lead – when she shows two ads on education. That same margin appears when Wilson tries to inoculate by talking about a mix of crime and the economy. When Brown attempts to inoculate showing a mix of crime and education or the economy and crime, the strategies produce a dead heat and a nine-point lead, respectively. Wilson talking only about crime or Wilson mixing a message with immigration and the economy also led to dead heats.

Pooling these different combinations of messages gives us an overall estimate of the ineffectiveness of inoculation as a campaign communication strategy. The same technique employed in the dialogue experiment (see Table 5.4) reveals the average penalty from replacing a commercial discussing a message favorable to a candidate with an ad concerning a topic favorable to the opponent. The attempt at inoculation, on average, costs the sponsoring candidate sixteen percentage points in the trial heat. This effect is statistically significant at the .1 level.

Table 5.4   *Inoculation Experiment: Strategies' Overall Effect on Vote*

Inoculate	−.16*
	(.09)
Subject's party	.49***
	(.06)
(Constant)	.15
N	197
Adj. R-square	26.6%

Note: Entries are OLS regression coefficients with standard errors in parentheses. Asterisks represent approximate significance levels: *** = $p < .01$; ** = $p < .05$; * = $p < .1$.

In sum, the experimental evidence is consistent with the model. The choice to dialogue costs the candidate. The choice to inoculate, which leads to dialogue, also results in a penalty. With regard to the governor's race, the evidence highlights Brown's mistake. Her decision to dialogue led to a net loss of electoral support, probably sufficient in concert with other factors to sway the course of the election. The evidence with respect to the broader theory will be interpreted more thoroughly below.

SURVEY EVIDENCE

I will briefly introduce another type of empirical data to support my contentions concerning Brown's loss. Experimental designs, while strong in terms of identifying causal agents, have their weaknesses. Because the experiments reported on in Table 5.5 and others were conducted under a particular set of conditions, it is possible that the results obtained will not apply to other populations, times or settings (Campbell and Stanley 1967). The small number of subjects provides a minimal base, thus limiting the power of statistical inferences. Finally, the short exposures (thirty-second spots) are not perfectly analogous to the flow of information campaigns generate in the real world. For these reasons, I include an aggregate analysis of this race based on sample surveys to strengthen the experimental findings.

The Field Institute regularly surveyed California's population during the period prior to the election. Taken together, these polls chart the

Table 5.5 *Survey Results: 1994 California Races*

Date	Gov. Vote		Brown's		Prop. 184 Vote			Yes
	Wilson	Brown	Und.	Share	Yes	No	Und.	Share
February 1–8, 1993	286	414	95	60%		-N/A-		
May 14–22, 1993	256	450	145	64%		-N/A-		
August 12–18, 1993	287	369	107	56%		-N/A-		
October 8–15, 1993	254	326	128	56%		-N/A-		
January 9–15, 1994	264	323	110	55%	585	65	47	90%
April 1–9, 1994	332	412	88	55%	318	74	24	81%
May 11–16, 1994	344	355	59	51%		-N/A-		
July 12–17, 1994	241	265	102	52%	200	73	39	73%
September 13–18, 1994	277	233	58	46%	351	139	84	72%
October 21–30, 1994	473	388	75	45%	650	284	89	70%

effect of the campaign on the electorate. Two questions play a paramount role in the analysis presented here. How will you vote for governor, and how will you vote on Proposition 184, the three-strikes initiative? The latter question serves as a proxy for the respondent's overall attitude on crime. The raw survey data are presented in Table 5.5.

In the aggregate, the line describing Brown's support is quite stark. Over the roughly twenty-one months prior to the election her support declined in a nearly linear fashion, from roughly 60 percent twenty-two months out to only 45 percent in the period prior to election day. This represents an unmistakable downward trend in her share of the vote.

The critical issue revolves around the cause of this decline. My model holds that the decline is a function of the dialogue on crime. This dialogue, in turn, should have primed the electorate to weight crime more heavily in vote choice. This priming effect would then work to Wilson's advantage, given the proximity of his stance to that of the median voter. The only available measure of the public's attitudes toward crime concerned respondents' vote intentions on Proposition 184. To test the priming hypothesis in these data, I estimated one regression model for each survey in order to chart the strength of the relationship between crime attitudes and the gubernatorial vote. The Proposition 184 question was only asked on five surveys. (The raw data appear in Table 5.5.)

The particular specification follows the same estimation technique employed in the experimental analyses. Partisan identification is in-

Table 5.6   *Survey Results: Relationship of Prop. 184 and Gubernatorial Votes*

Date	Prop. 184 Vote	Partisan ID	Constant	Adj. R-sq.	N
January 9–15, 1994	.05*	.41***	.07	.20	1,007
April 1–9, 1994	.11***	.56***	.07	.29	1,009
July 12–17, 1994	.13***	.49***	.03	.28	846
September 13–18, 1994	.19***	.40***	−.01	.23	854
October 21–30, 1994	.25***	.45***	−.02	.30	1,403

Note: Entries are OLS regression coefficients from an equation that estimated respondents' gubernatorial vote from their partisan identification and their intended Proposition 184 vote. Asterisks represent approximate significance levels: *** = $p < .01$; * = $p < .1$.

cluded as a baseline for comparison and as a control given the well-established effect of partisan feelings on vote choice (Miller and Shanks 1996; Converse and Markus 1979; Campbell et al. 1960). The estimates produced by the five regression specifications appear in Table 5.6. As we can see, the effect of respondents' positions on Proposition 184 on the gubernatorial vote steadily increased while the effect of partisanship remained relatively constant. In January of 1994, the effect of crime attitudes was minimal; the coefficient was .05, significant at the .1 level, which means there was a slightly positive relationship between attitudes concerning crime and the vote for governor.

By the end of the campaign in October of 1994, there was a very strong relationship between these two choices. In fact, the coefficient on Proposition 184 is over half the size of the coefficient on partisanship, .25 and .45 respectively, meaning the strength of the influence of crime attitudes was comparable to that of partisanship, the paramount political construct. In all, during the period of the campaign, the importance of crime attitudes in determining the vote rose almost linearly just as Brown's support was declining at the same rate. Figure 5.2 charts this relationship. While the survey data do not allow the direction of causality to be established, it is consistent with the experimental results.

INTERPRETATION AND SUMMARY

We have two sets of empirical results, one that supports the mechanics underlying my theoretical model, and one that verifies the model's

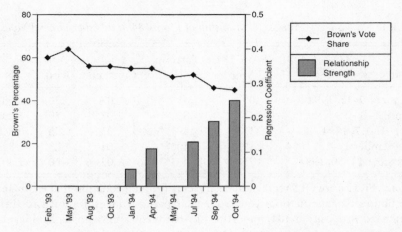

Figure 5.2   Survey results: Brown's vote share and weight of crime attitudes.

primary result. I will briefly summarize the empirical data and then place these studies into perspective using my game-theoretic approach.

The empirical premises of the model all concern the effect of campaign communications on the voters. In the experimental results presented in this and the previous chapter, I have verified two important assumptions. First, every ad, regardless of its sponsor, serves to increase the salience of that ad's theme in the voter's mind. Familiarity with the research discussed in chapter four would have led one to expect this priming effect to appear. Second, advertisements seem to inform voters of the candidates' positions with respect to their content, without altering either the voters' attitudes concerning that subject or changing the voters' perceptions of candidates' attitudes and stances toward that subject. In other words, also consistent with the literature, ads lead to opinionation but not to learning or persuasion. These two effects of campaign communication form the basis of my formal model.

The model's primary prediction is that the candidates' strategic calculus will eliminate the prospect of campaign dialogue in the real world. The two-ad experiments verify this result by demonstrating the penalties imposed on the candidate who attempts to dialogue. On average, an ad devoted to dialogue cost the candidate one-fifth of an average vote compared to the best possible response, at least among these respondents. Similarly, an ad devoted to inoculation, a dialogue-enhancing message-creation strategy, typically cost the candidate one-sixth of

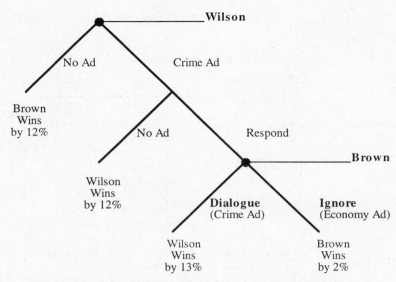

Figure 5.3 One-ad and dialogue experiment: Sample decision tree.

a vote on average, relative to a dialogue-diminishing strategy. These penalties may be somewhat exaggerated due to the experimental context, but it is clear that candidates seeking to win an election would be acting against their self-interest by adopting either form of dialogue-enhancing strategy when creating their messages.

Returning to the 1994 California gubernatorial experiments in more detail illustrates this point. The experimental results allow us to reconstruct the options available to each candidate whenever he or she made a strategic decision in the message construction process. Thus, they allow a more thorough analysis of each candidate's strategic calculation, which, in turn, reveals the intuition behind the dialogue hypothesis. I will first explicate the candidate's reasoning in the case of crime, and then point out how the same logic carries over to all other dimensions. Figure 5.3 summarizes this illustration.

Four different scenarios are necessary to capture the logic underlying the candidates' decisions with respect to crime. They are labeled control, crime, dialogue, and ignore. These scenarios correspond to experimental conditions for which we have a known result. Control, for example, postulates no message construction or dissemination. The subject population's partisanship is slightly skewed toward the Democratic party, much like the partisanship of California in 1994. As would

Initiating Candidate and Issue:

Response:		Wilson Crime	Brown Economy	Brown Education
(Brown or Wilson)	Crime	loses by 13%	wins by 5%	wins by 13%
	Immigration		loses by 5%	loses by 9%
	Economy	wins by 2%	loses by 26%	
	Education	tie		loses by 9%

Figure 5.4 Dialogue experiment: "Payoff" matrix (underlined responses represent dialogue attempts). *Note: Entries are electoral outcomes from the responding candidate's perspective.*

be expected with this skew and normal party voting, Brown wins in the control or no exposure condition. Specifically, as the one-ad experiment indicates, she wins by 12 percent. The other three conditions represent other scenarios. Treatment represents subjects exposed to only a Wilson crime ad. The remaining scenarios are taken from the two-ad experiments. In dialogue, subjects see a Wilson crime ad and a Brown crime ad, while in ignore, subjects see a Wilson crime ad and a Brown economy ad.

In my reconstruction of the decisions that produce a campaign, I am temporarily assuming that the choices are ordered so that each candidate chooses between a particular set of scenarios in a particular sequence. Figure 5.3 presents one possible set of decisions predicated on the assumption that Wilson chooses or moves first. Note, I place no theoretical importance on the first-mover/second-mover distinction; however, assuming Wilson moves first serves to clarify the counterfactuals with respect to this illustration. As first mover, Wilson is faced with the choice of advertising or not advertising. As a practical matter, this choice is uninteresting, but in theory, at least, it represents Wilson's choice of themes and his strategic calculations. Facing a loss of twelve percentage points, perhaps representing his low initial public standing, he will opt for a crime ad. Were the game to stop here, after the incumbent aired his crime message, as it does for many underfinanced challengers, Wilson would win by twelve percentage points. The more theoretically interesting choice is Brown's: She can dialogue by showing a crime ad or she can ignore by showing an ad on the economy. Here Brown is faced with a twelve-point loss or a marginal (two-point) win. As an instrumentally rational actor, she should select the ignore response with the economy ad. Thus, in this particular branch of the tree, dialogue is a dominated strategy and it is only because of the Brown campaign's misplaced strategic direction that we witnessed it in the real world. Therein lays Brown's mistake and the "point in the road where the campaign went south."

The undesirability of dialogue from the candidate's perspective is reiterated in the rest of the experimental results. Figure 5.4 presents this reinterpretation of data from the two-ad experiment. No matter who the initiating candidate and no matter what the issue, the dialogue response is always the least desirable for the opposing candidate. There are other interesting points highlighted by this arrangement of the data, most notably the unrealized success of education as an issue for Brown, but the main point is clear – dialogue does not win.

CHAPTER 6

Dialogue and Its Effects in Contemporary American Elections

Having linked dialogue to democratic legitimacy, I have identified the forces that discourage candidates from adopting dialogue-enhancing strategies. These theoretical understandings of the candidates' incentive structures were developed into a two-player game that models campaigns in mass elections. The game focuses on candidates' strategic choices over what to discuss in campaigns. In the last chapter, a case study of the 1994 California gubernatorial race tested this model. Taken together, the model and the case study show that the choice to dialogue will likely lead to electoral defeat. Now attention can be devoted to a broader study of dialogue in U.S. Senate campaigns. In the next chapter, I will refine the model in order to develop and test predictions concerning the appearance of dialogue in these races. This second step will advance the ultimate goal of promoting better campaign discourse. This chapter takes on the first step in the Senate study – an examination of campaigning as it naturally occurs.

Senate elections present a superior set of situations to further study the dynamics underlying dialogue. In the first place, they present a larger number of cases, in a given time, than any comparable race. At least thirty-three senate elections happen in every cycle. In contrast, the United States has undertaken the process of electing a president only seventeen times since World War II. At the same time, unlike elections to the House of Representatives, where the majority of elections are effectively decided prior to the campaign, senate elections generally have two carefully orchestrated and reasonably financed campaigns. Nevertheless, the variation in the character of these races still provides a scientific advantage.

A wide range of candidate pairings and environments present themselves in the races to be examined here. Perhaps for this reason, the

National Election Studies (NES) conducted a set of senate voter surveys, the Senate Election Study (SES), which is particularly valuable. In this study, a small but nearly representative sample of voters was interviewed in each race in the 1988, 1990, and 1992 election cycles. My study of senate campaigns extends only to these cycles for this reason. Moreover, the diversity in the positions taken by senate candidates in these elections will be critical to applying and refining the model in the next chapter. The variation in the level of dialogue produced by these forces will be useful in assessing dialogue's effects, as well.

The model of campaigns in mass elections presented in chapter four leads us to believe that little if any dialogue will appear in contemporary campaigns. This chapter's analyses of forty-nine races supplement the case study in testing this basic prediction. In addition, the beneficial effects of what dialogue occurs will be assessed, using survey measures developed by political behavior researchers. Examining a broader set of cases generally produces more confidence in a finding. In moving from one race to almost fifty, however, some depth must be sacrificed. Instead of relying on an experimental design, the following analyses are based primarily on content analysis. While this method lacks the rigorous test of causality that is the hallmark of experimentation, this technique does have advantages. To start, the observations of campaigns take place almost as they occur in the real world, so content analysis eliminates some of the artificiality of experimentation.

Most important, while the experiment took dialogue as a dichotomy – the exposure to the candidates' ads either did or did not feature dialogue – the content analysis of dialogue employs a continuous measure, departing from the all-or-nothing approach. This leads to a more precise examination because the level of dialogue in each race can be charted. The new measure creates the opportunity to make comparisons – to look, for example, at what causes dialogue. The continuous nature of this measure is also suitable for a quick look at dialogue's effects on the quality of voting, which will be presented after a review of the methodology, procedures, and a description of the results.

METHODOLOGY

This study requires the measurement of campaign discourse, and it shares the same basic procedures as all content analyses. Prior to observation, the scope of the study must be established and a suitable coding scheme developed. Coding schemes are essentially recipes for translating raw input into an appropriate dataset. With a scope and a scheme, researchers assemble the raw data and make observations in the form of codes. While coding, they read or view the content and categorize it according to the scheme. There are several requirements to doing this successfully, which I shall discuss as I report on my application.

Coding is always done with an eye toward a particular research question, so the primary test of a scheme's adequacy is its ability to provide useful information. This study asks how much dialogue occurs in campaigns, creating a measurement need that motivates my scheme. In addition, a tradeoff exists between the complexity of a scheme and the amount of content that can be coded given available resources. I wished to examine a reasonably large number of races in this study, so the coding scheme had to be relatively simple as well as efficient.

Given a focus on dialogue in senate races, the scope was initially driven by the availability of content. The problem with much campaign research is the absence of direct information on what the candidates say. To study dialogue, it would be ideal to have recordings of exactly what the candidates and their managers publicly discussed at each point in the campaign. Alternatively, a possibly superior measure could be constructed by accurately registering what a sample of voters heard during the campaign season. In the absence of these kinds of records, I have chosen to examine newspaper coverage as a surrogate for the campaign-generated information flow.

Newspapers provide a better measure than candidates' advertisements because they take a more holistic and exhaustive view. Sometimes, in the aftermath of the election, even if one can find all the advertisements produced by a campaign, it is hard to tell how much an ad was run, or even if it ran at all. Likewise, scholars have argued that the newspaper details the best information available to the voter during the campaign season. Because they do not expect the voters to read all the coverage, they claim that a content analysis of newspaper reports measures the ceiling over what voters could acquire if they paid attention to everything (Westlye 1991). In other words, this measure should be thought of as an "upper bound" on voter knowledge. If analyzed properly, newspaper coverage should provide an adequate indicator of the amount of dialogue in a campaign.

More pragmatically, newspapers are becoming increasingly easy to analyze efficiently. Unlike speeches or television broadcasts, newspapers are intended to be permanent records. As we continue into the information age, these records can be accessed digitally and can be transferred and downloaded in a relatively short time. The nature of this data also significantly increases coding reliability and efficiency.

DATA SELECTION ASSEMBLY AND CODING

For this analysis, every digital archive then publicly available was searched for full-text copies of the newspapers covering the 1988, 1990, and 1992 senate races. Ultimately, three archives were used – *Lexis-Nexis*, *Datatimes*, and *Dialog* (*Westlaw*). In states represented by more than one paper, the one with the largest circulation was selected. In all, fifty-one races meet the criteria for this form of analysis. The races, associated papers, candidates, and a race code combining the state and year, (for instance "AZ88") are presented in Table 6.1.

Table 6.1 *Races Included in the Analyses of Senate Campaigns*

State	Newspaper	Republican	Democrat	Code
AZ	*Arizona Republic*	DeGreen	DeConcini	AZ88
CA	*Los Angeles Times*	Wilson	McCarthy	CA88
FL	*St. Petersburg Times*	Mack	MacKay	FL88
MA	*Boston Globe*	Malone	Kennedy	MA88
MI	*Detroit Free Press*	Dunn	Riegle	MI88
MN	*Minneapolis Star Tribune*	Durenberger	Humphrey	MN88
MO	*St. Louis Post-Dispatch*	Danforth	Nixon	MO88
NE	*Omaha World-Herald*	Karnes	Kerrey	NE88
NJ	*New Jersey Record*	Dawkins	Lautenberg	NJ88
NY	*New York Times*	McMillan	Moynihan	NY88
OH	*Columbus Dispatch*	Voinovich	Metzenbaum	OH88
TX	*Dallas Morning News*	Boutler	Bentsen	TX88
WA	*Seattle Times*	Gorton	Lowry	WA88
CO	*Rocky Mountain News*	Brown	Heath	CO90
IL	*Chicago Tribune*	Martin	Simon	IL90
IN	*Indianapolis News*	Coats	Hill	IN90
KS	*Wichita Eagle*	Kassebaum	Williams	KS90
KY	*Courier-Journal*	McConnell	Sloane	KY90
MA	*Boston Globe*	Rappaport	Kerry	MA90
MI	*Detroit Free Press*	Schuette	Levin	MI90
MN	*Minneapolis Star Tribune*	Boschwitz	Wellstone	MN90
NC	*Charlotte Observer*	Helms	Gantt	NC90
NE	*Omaha World-Herald*	Daub	Exon	NE90

Table 6.1   (*cont.*)

State	Newspaper	Republican	Democrat	Code
NJ	*New Jersey Record*	Whitman	Bradley	NJ90
OK	*Tulsa Tribune/World*	Jones	Boren	OK90
OR	*Portland Oregonian*	Hatfield	Lonsdale	OR90
TX	*Dallas Morning News*	Gramm	Parmer	TX90
VA	*Richmond News Leader*	Warner	Spannaus	VA90
AZ	*Arizona Republic*	McCain	Sargent	AZ92
CO	*Rocky Mountain News*	Considine	Campbell	CO92
CT	*Hartford Courant*	Johnson	Dodd	CT92
FL	*St. Petersburg Times*	Grant	Graham	FL92
GA	*Atlanta Constitution*	Coverdell	Fowler Jr.	GA92
IA	*Des Moines Register*	Grassley	Lloyd-Jones	IA92
IL	*Chicago Tribune*	Williamson	Braun	IL92
IN	*Indianapolis News*	Coats	Hogsett	IN92
KS	*Kansas City Star*	Dole	O'Dell	KS92
KY	*Courier-Journal*	Williams	Ford	KY92
MD	*Baltimore Sun*	Keyes	Mikulski	MD92
MO	*St. Louis Post-Dispatch*	Bond	Rothman-Serot	MO92
NC	*Charlotte Observer*	Faircloth	Sanford	NC92
NV	*Las Vegas Review-Journal*	Dahl	Reid	NV92
NY	*New York Times*	D'Amato	Abrams	NY92
OH	*Columbus Dispatch*	DeWine	Glenn	OH92
OK	*Tulsa Tribune/World*	Nickles	Lewis	OK92
OR	*Portland Oregonian*	Packwood	AuCoin	OR92
PA	*Philadelphia Inquirer*	Specter	Lynn	PA92
WA	*Seattle Times*	Chandler	Murray	WA92
WI	*Milwaukee Journal/ Sentinel*	Kasten	Feingold	WI92

In 1992 California had two senate races – Dianne Feinstein against John Seymour and Barbara Boxer against Bruce Herschensohn. The coverage of these races proved difficult to disentangle, so they were excluded from the analyses, leaving forty-nine races. As Table 6.2 points out the sample differs systematically from all the senate races in this period in a few regards.

As expected, there are statistically significant differences in the average level of expenditures, the size of the voting age population and in the percentage of urban residents across these two groups. On the other hand, the rest of the indicators are all quite comparable, and we

Table 6.2 *Comparison of Races Included to All Senate Races*

	Sampled Races	All Races
Expenditures	7,378,541.574	5,549,721.39**
Ratio of expenditures	6.9377	6.124
Voting age Population	5,816,418.18	3,813,295.24***
Unemployment	5.878	5.77
Percent with college	24.815	25.018
Percent urban	73.622	68.407**
Average age	33.058	32.775
Percent white	81.569	82.109
Percent black	9.808	8.877
Percent Latin	6.487	5.27
N	49	105

Note: Asterisks indicate levels of statistical significance: ***p < .01; **p < .05; *p < .1.

have enough variation within the sample to overcome the observed differences.

The actual content analysis was conducted in two stages. In the first stage the full-text of every article that ran after Labor Day and before the election that mentioned either candidate was downloaded. This procedure was repeated at least twice for every race, with every unique article passed to the second stage. Table 6.3 summarizes the amount of articles coded in each race as well as some other information that will be discussed below. At the second stage, the articles were loaded into databases accessible with personal computers. Using customized software, trained coders read one article at a time.

The coder first decided whether the article should be coded. Not all articles downloaded were relevant to the study. For example, the *Chicago Tribune* carried many articles relating to Paul Simon (the singer, not the senator), these and similar articles were discarded. Having decided that the article should be coded, the coder then observed the percentage of the article relevant to the campaign from the voters' perspective. This percentage was expressed in lines, which were standardized by

Table 6.3   *Details on Total, Horserace, and Substantive Coverage by Race*

	Available			Percent			
Code	Articles	Coded	Horserace	Horserace	Substance	Other	Candidates
AZ88	115	6,446	3,154	48	3,292	2,087	1,205
CA88	100	8,955	3,966	44	4,989	2,510	2,479
FL88	145	12,213	7,619	62	4,594	2,790	1,804
MA88	58	2,695	964	35	1,731	727	1,004
MI88	55	3,966	2,927	73	1,039	770	269
MN88	168	11,353	6,285	55	5,068	2,523	2,545
MO88	116	5,600	3,074	54	2,526	1,802	724
NE88	307	25,291	13,428	53	11,863	7,427	4,436
NJ88	91	7,247	5,281	72	1,966	809	1,157
NY88	67	2,266	476	21	1,790	855	935
OH88	60	4,610	2,818	61	1,792	880	912
TX88	191	9,467	5,422	57	4,045	2,550	1,495
WA88	178	15,908	9,926	62	5,982	3,946	2,036
CO90	137	9,351	4,763	50	4,588	3,153	1,435
IL90	129	5,083	2,348	46	2,735	1,614	1,121
IN90	73	5,654	2,776	49	2,878	1,685	1,193
KS90	59	1,687	427	25	1,260	754	506
KY90	220	19,591	11,144	56	8,447	5,566	2,881
MA90	143	12,979	7,811	60	5,168	2,148	3,020
MI90	110	9,465	4,798	50	4,667	3,491	1,176
MN90	202	14,149	8,058	56	6,091	3,700	2,391
NC90	368	28,619	11,932	41	16,687	11,485	5,202
NE90	170	12,570	6,280	49	6,290	2,956	3,334
NJ90	89	4,954	2,834	57	2,120	1,197	923
OK90	84	3,718	967	26	2,751	1,244	1,507
OR90	176	25,915	15,229	58	10,686	6,089	4,597
TX90	98	4,019	2,221	55	1,798	760	1,038
VA90	75	2,937	884	30	2,053	1,429	624
AZ92	191	8,843	4,020	45	4,823	2,454	2,369
CO92	173	14,384	7,245	50	7,139	4,227	2,912
CT92	105	10,429	5,988	57	4,441	2,633	1,808
FL92	74	3,339	1,806	54	1,533	942	591
GA92	92	5,122	2,906	56	2,216	1,222	994
IA92	109	4,508	1,789	39	2,719	1,925	794
IL92	154	14,508	7,598	52	6,910	4,341	2,569
IN92	57	4,968	2,007	40	2,961	1,207	1,754
KS92	75	2,553	1,023	40	1,530	923	607
KY92	72	4,008	2,525	62	1,483	1,273	210
MD92	81	4,619	1,856	40	2,763	1,496	1,267
MO92	66	4,384	1,815	41	2,569	1,772	797
NC92	118	8,261	4,139	50	4,122	2,230	1,892

Table 6.3   (*cont.*)

Code	Available			Percent			
	Articles	Coded	Horserace	Horserace	Substance	Other	Candidates
NV92	137	6,364	3,381	53	2,983	2,031	952
NY92	177	18,146	11,512	63	6,634	4,510	2,124
OH92	88	6,779	3,397	50	3,382	2,005	1,377
OK92	121	4,775	1,137	23	3,638	1,565	2,073
OR92	218	13,207	5,845	44	7,362	4,319	3,043
PA92	183	23,361	11,943	51	11,418	6,825	4,593
WA92	108	7,276	3,768	51	3,508	2,814	694
WI92	176	16,073	9,398	58	6,675	2,617	4,058
Total	6,359	462,615	242,910		219,705	130,278	89,427
Minimum	55	1,687	427	21	1,039	727	210
Maximum	368	28,619	15,229	73	16,687	11,485	5,202
Average	129	9,441	4,957	52	4,483	2,658	1,825

Microsoft FoxPro, the database software used. These lines are roughly equivalent to a line in a double newspaper column. The relevant content was placed into one of thirty-three categories, which are discussed below. Most articles fit into more than one category and up to five categories were coded for each article. Then for each category, the amount and source of the material was noted. Coders made additional observations, which will be discussed as appropriate.

DIMENSIONS OF THE INFORMATION FLOW

The point of the coding scheme was to capture the content of the information flow and its sources for use in subsequent analyses. To review, I defined a dimension or theme as anything a candidate can discuss that potentially affects an individual's vote. My notion includes traditional issues like abortion and gun control, as well as less concrete topics such as questions of character, policy, or ideology. The definition also limited the number of potential dimensions and reduced idiosyncrasies by taking the candidates' perspective and looking at topics more generally. For example, abortion includes the ideas of choice as well as the right-to-life. This definition of dimension presents the candidate with clear strategic choice of themes in message construction. Specifically, should they devote their communication budget to talking about this or that theme? Thus, the coding scheme must first define all the subjects the candidates could discuss.

The list of dimensions was created iteratively. At the beginning, intuition and experience yielded a list of many possible dimensions. Extensive piloting was done on random samples of articles. Dimensions were added and combined until nearly every text portion could be coded and the boundaries between dimensions were clear. The dimensions discussed below are a putatively exhaustive list of the themes candidates can discuss; there was a small miscellaneous category for things that could not be coded. The amount of material coded as miscellaneous was small, about 3.5 percent. The dimensions, presented in Table 6.4 (along with shorter coding designators, like "abort") are discussed in the remainder of this section.

With the list of thirty-three dimensions complete, the coding began in earnest. To make training and coding easier, the dimensions were discussed in terms of classes of categories, including the strategic dimension, issue dimensions, broader dimensions, and character dimensions. The discussion follows these groupings, proceeding alphabetically in each. These distinctions between dimensions do not play a role in subsequent analyses. The strategic dimension does however demand some special attention. This content, commonly known as horserace coverage, deals with the strategic aspects of the campaign that the media are fond of covering, but relates only indirectly to the candidates' discussion. This category was also not used in further analyses but is discussed first along with some statistics on the total amount of material coded.

TOTAL COVERAGE AND THE STRATEGIC DIMENSION

In all 6,359 articles were coded with almost a half a million FoxPro lines (462,615 exactly) judged to be relevant to the campaigns. Table 6.3 presents these data broken down by race. On average there were 129 articles and 9,441 lines per race. The 1990 North Carolina race between Gant and Helms produced the most – 368 articles with 28,619 lines. The 1988 Michigan race between Dunn and Riegle produced the fewest articles with 55 and the 1990 Kansas race between O'Dell and Dole produced the fewest lines with 1,687. Of the total, 13,746 lines were not categorized – the miscellaneous category of about 3.5 percent.

The media, including newspapers, generally cover campaigns using a frame or template widely known as the horserace, as discussed in previous chapters. Strategic aspects of the campaign, such as who is leading, who has more money, and who is showing more effective commercials, play a prominent role in this kind of coverage. In many

Table 6.4   *The Information Flow's Dimensions*

Category	Number	Dimension Horserace	Code
Strategic	1	Abortion	ABORT
Issue	2	Agriculture	FARMS
	3	Civil rights	CIVRTS
	4	Crime	CRIME
	5	Defense	DEFEND
	6	Economy	ECON
	7	Education	EDUC
	8	Environment	ENVIRON
	9	Foreign policy	FORPOL
	10	Health care	HEALTH
	11	Immigration	IMMIG
	12	NAFTA/Trade	TRADE
	13	Regulation	REGS
	14	Scandal	SCANDAL
	15	Social Security	SOCSEC
	16	Spending/Deficit	SPEND
	17	Taxes	TAX
	18	Welfare	WELF
	19	Women's issues	WOMEN
Broader Issue	20	Bringing back Federal money	PORK
	21	Conservative	CON
	22	Flip Flop	FLIP
	23	Government gridlock	GRID
	24	Liberal	LIB
	25	Performance in office	PERF
	26	Religion/Family values	RELIG
	27	Special interests/PACS	PACS
	28	Washington insider/ Out of touch	WASH
Character	29	Biography	BIO
	30	Competence	COMP
	31	Integrity	INTEG
	32	Personality	PERSON

instances, reporters weave horserace coverage into information about what the candidates stand for or are doing. For example, when a candidate gives a speech on a particular topic, the reporter may add information on why the candidate chose that topic as well as information on the race's background, such as the latest opinion poll.

By using this frame, as many scholars have pointed out, the media promote the view that they are unbiased handicappers. This frame also supplies easy to gather doses of material during the ongoing campaign. This style is also more dramatic, which can increase ratings. Thus, from the media's standpoint, coverage of the campaign as a horserace has substantial benefits (Gitlin 1983; Patterson 1993; Capella and Jamieson 1997). On the other hand, horserace coverage has little relevance to the ongoing study. It can be viewed as padding, because its influence on what the voters can learn from the campaign is limited. The strategic issue category was used to track and isolate horserace coverage. Coders were instructed to place content that treated "discussions of the campaign as a political sport," such as answers to questions like, "Who is winning, and is the lead widening?" as well as related material – campaign finance reports, candidate targeting strategies, and the like – in this category.

Consistent with other studies of horserace journalism, the amount of attention devoted to the strategic dimension in these campaigns was quite high. The left-hand column of Table 6.3 presents the total amount of coverage in articles as well as lines and, moving rightward, the amount of horserace and substantive coverage in each race. Slightly over half of the material (52 percent or 242,910 lines) was coded as strategic. The amount of horserace coverage did, however, differ across races. At the lower end, the 1988 New York race (McMillan *vs.* Moynihan) had just one in five lines, 21 percent, devoted to horserace aspects, while at the upper end, the 1988 Michigan race (Dunn *vs.* Riegle) had 73 percent. Figure 6.1 graphically details the distribution of these percentages. The bulk of the races (forty-one) fell between 43 and 65 percent of horserace coverage while, of the remainder, six had less and two had more than this percentage of horserace coverage.

All further analyses are conducted on the content remaining after the exclusion of horserace coverage. The amounts of this kind of coverage are shown in the sixth column of Table 6.3. Because nonhorserace coverage totals are nothing more than total coverage minus that accorded to the strategic dimension, the topic requires no further discussion.

When people speak about political issues, especially candidates taking positions, they generally refer to the somewhat limited set of

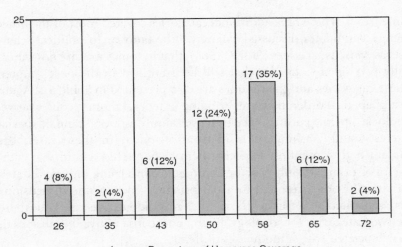

Figure 6.1 Distribution of horserace coverage by race.

policy areas contested in contemporary politics. This coding scheme identified fifteen of these dimensions. In alphabetical order they are: abortion, agriculture, civil rights, crime/drugs, defense, economy, education, environment, foreign policy, health care, immigration, NAFTA/trade, Social Security, spending, Welfare, and women's issues. A shorter code name was also assigned to ease data analysis and the explication of results. These names are given on the right side of Table 6.4.

Some of the categories combined two closely related ideas because one of the ideas by itself didn't have enough material to form a clearly separable category, for example crime/drugs and NAFTA/trade each contained two nearly distinct themes that, in practice, were inseparable. Collapsing any two categories into one works against the no dialogue prediction, if only because the candidates have fewer discussion options. In other cases, there was enough distinct content to merit adding a category. Spending included all references to the federal deficit, which many candidates discussed in 1992 and did not fit well elsewhere. For many categories a boundary-defining rule was established to ease coding. Any mention of the military, for instance, was coded as defense, unless it specifically involved a foreign location, like Haiti, in which case it was also coded as foreign policy. Remember a single article could have been coded in up to five categories.

These issue categories did not go far enough in capturing the candidates' rhetoric, so others were added under the heading broader dimensions. These nine additional categories covered most of the other themes candidates discussed. Many will be familiar to political scientists as consensual issues (Stokes 1966), that is, topics that are not inherently two-sided – an idea that will be examined in the next chapter. These categories and their names are also presented in Table 6.4. Again in alphabetical order, they are: bringing in federal money, conservative, gridlock, liberal, performance, religion/family values, scandal, special interests, and Washington insider/out-of-touch. In these cases, the content had to mention a specific item to be placed within that category. For example, only specific comments concerning one candidate's activities in office resulted in a performance code. Some dimensions were separated because the describing items did not overlap. Thus there are two categories for ideology, liberal and conservative, because each was associated with a unique set of items.

Finally, the information flow contained some discussion of character. Four categories were used here. Any discussion of adjectives or facts that could be used to describe a candidate was placed in these categories. They are competence, integrity, personality, and biography. The adjectives intelligent, honest, and dull, for example, respectively fit into each of these categories. The first two categories correspond to labels long used by political scientists to code traits. The third and fourth categories were added to provide a more complete view of character in light of coding experience.

SOURCES AND COVERAGE ACROSS DIMENSIONS

Information about the content's sources was recovered from the substantive material while coding. To make the coding scheme as accurate as possible, only direct quotes from or content attributed to a candidate or member of a campaign team were coded as originating from a campaign. All other content was placed in an "other" category, as reported in Table 6.3. Of the 219,705 lines, 89,427 were assigned to one of the candidates in the race, over 40 percent. These lines are the bases for measuring dialogue in the campaign.

There are, as expected, considerable differences in thematic selection across races; nevertheless there are some commonalties. Table 6.5 presents a summary of all substantive discussion as well as its sources.

Figure 6.2 shows the totals graphically. Of the thirty-two dimensions, performance, environment, and economy were the ones most discussed, while immigration, gridlock, and personality were the ones least

Table 6.5 *Summary of Coverage by Dimension*

Code	Total	Other Sources	Candidates	Percent Candidates	Percent Rank
PORK	2,472	1,543	929	38	21
CON	2,517	1,372	1,145	45	15
FLIP	2,387	1,633	754	32	27
GRID	1,053	298	755	72	1
LIB	5,472	1,772	3,700	68	2
PERF	25,552	18,267	7,285	29	29
RELIG	2,574	1,286	1,288	50	9
PACS	12,401	8,366	4,035	33	26
WASH	4,259	2,198	2,061	48	11
BIO	4,243	3,508	735	17	33
COMP	2,664	1,970	694	26	30
INTEG	8,289	4,329	3,960	48	12
PERSON	2,143	1,645	498	23	32
ABORT	9,874	6,710	3,164	32	28
FARMS	2,254	979	1,275	57	3
CIVRTS	5,908	3,727	2,181	37	23
CRIME	8,678	4,277	4,401	51	7
DEFEND	8,895	5,219	3,676	41	18
ECON	12,747	6,377	6,370	50	10
EDUC	4,405	2,279	2,126	48	13
ENVIRON	16,533	9,794	6,739	41	19
FORPOL	7,386	4,573	2,813	38	22
HEALTH	8,791	3,820	4,971	57	4
IMMIG	177	108	69	39	20
LOCAL	6,333	4,163	2,170	34	25
TRADE	3,541	1,701	1,840	52	6
REGS	3,012	2,224	788	26	31
SCANDAL	4,503	2,017	2,486	55	5
SOCSEC	4,544	2,609	1,935	43	17
SPEND	10,326	5,745	4,581	44	16
TAX	10,922	5,825	5,097	47	14
WELF	2,447	1,195	1,252	51	8
WOMEN	4,990	3,224	1,766	35	24
Total	212,292	124,753	87,539	0	
Minimum	177	108	69	17	
Maximum	25,552	18,267	7,285	72	
Average	6,433.1	3,780.4	2,652.7	42	

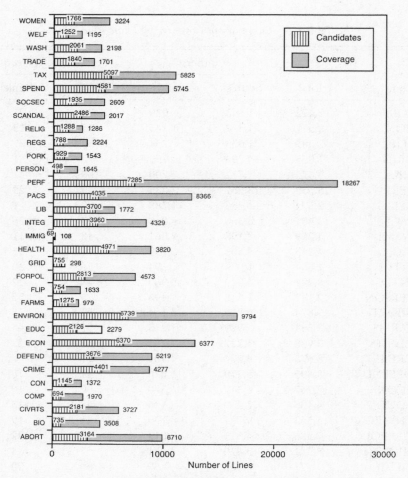

Figure 6.2 Amount of candidate discussion and total coverage by dimension.

discussed, for all sources. Not surprisingly, the order for content attributed to the candidates matched these rankings. For candidates, performance, environment, and the economy were the three dimensions discussed most and immigration, personality, and competence were the three dimensions least discussed. To give us some idea of the balancing of sources used in coverage, the proportion of material attributed to the candidates can also be used to rank the dimensions.

In Figure 6.2, we see that the candidates talked more of the time in the cases of gridlock, liberal, and health care while they talked least about the character dimensions of biography, personality, and competence. In short, at least so far, it seems that the results of the content analysis accord with our intuitions about the information flow's contents, not to mention the candidates' desires with respect to thematic selection.

MEASURING DIALOGUE

Returning to the main point, the content data need to be rearranged to construct a measure of dialogue. Taking the codes as an indicator of who said what in the course of a campaign provides two potential measures. First, dialogue can be seen as an immediate occurrence, which I will call instant dialogue. Instant dialogue appears immediately in the sense that it occurs within an article. This measure is closer to the way dialogue is used in the experimental design – either an article's content features dialogue or it does not. If it does not feature dialogue, the candidates are said to be ignoring each other. The indicator stems from a count of the number of articles, weighted by their length, with and without dialogue. For example, if an article discusses crime, and features points from both candidates, then the relevant numbers of lines are counted as instant dialogue. If only one candidate discussed crime then these lines are counted in the ignore column.

The second measure looks at the amount of dialogue over the course of the campaign, what I call sustained dialogue. The information on who said what during the course of the campaigns can be separated into content from the advantaged as opposed to the disadvantaged candidate. By definition, on a given dimension the advantaged candidate is speaking for the majority and the disadvantaged candidate is speaking for the minority. The sustained dialogue measure sums the amount of minority content across all dimensions for the campaign. The more the amount of minority information approaches the total amount of discussion, the more dialogue occurs. For instance, imagine two candidates discussing abortion over the course of a campaign. All the lines in a campaign in which a candidate discussed the majority opinion, which happens to be pro-choice in these elections, would fit in the majority column, that is, against dialogue. On the other hand, all the lines where the minority opinion was discussed would count as dissent, that is, toward dialogue.

The idea that no voter will read every article justifies the adoption of both measures. It does not seem too far-fetched to suppose that there is only a probability that, as they scan the paper, voters will read any single article relevant to the campaign. The likelihood of a voter's reading all the articles is quite small. Imagine, for instance, that there is a 95 percent chance – a very high probability – that a voter will read any specific article. Then, the chance of that voter seeing every article in a race with twenty articles is only .35 (.95 to the twentieth power). With 150 articles, the probability falls to less than .0005 (.95 raised to 150). Thus, dialogue is measured in two ways, which together will capture the electorate's exposure to dialogue from any one article as well as the amount of dialogue generated within the entire race. These two measures are also combined into a composite indicator for the analyses at the end of this chapter and the next.

LEVELS OF INSTANT AND SUSTAINED DIALOGUE IN U.S. SENATE CAMPAIGNS

As predicted, the level of instant dialogue is not high. Of the 89,427 substantive lines coded, only 17,439, or about twenty percent fall into this category. The remaining 71,988 lines are assessed for sustained dialogue below. The statistics for each race are presented in Table 6.6.

Table 6.6 *Instant and Sustained Dialogue Lines by Race*

Code	Candidates	Dialogue	Ignore	Instant Dialogue	Minority	Majority	Sustained Dialogue
AZ88	1,205	0	1,205	0	198	942	16
CA88	2,479	459	2,020	18	85	1,941	4
FL88	1,804	144	1,660	7	180	973	10
MA88	1,004	264	740	26	81	616	10
MI88	269	137	132	50	14	117	10
MN88	2,545	657	1,888	25	423	1,576	22
MO88	724	175	549	24	23	538	4
NE88	4,436	447	3,989	10	832	3,111	20
NJ88	1,157	164	993	14	84	771	8
NY88	935	289	646	30	48	594	7
OH88	912	161	751	17	52	666	6
TX88	1,495	0	1,495	0	257	1,384	17
WA88	2,036	681	1,355	33	362	959	26
CO90	1,435	690	745	48	30	715	4
IL90	1,121	101	1,020	9	112	880	10
IN90	1,193	259	934	21	45	937	4
KS90	506	124	382	24	24	361	6
KY90	2,881	563	2,318	19	471	1,907	20
MA90	3,020	601	2,419	19	459	1,421	18

Table 6.6   (*cont.*)

Code	Candidates	Dialogue	Ignore	Instant Dialogue	Minority	Majority	Sustained Dialogue
MI90	1,176	107	1,069	9	171	849	15
MN90	2,391	533	1,858	22	318	1,468	17
NC90	5,202	682	4,520	13	972	3,321	21
NE90	3,334	606	2,728	18	422	2,385	15
NJ90	923	208	715	22	25	691	3
OK90	1,507	0	1,507	0	103	1,516	6
OR90	4,597	754	3,843	16	495	3,371	12
TX90	1,038	117	921	11	49	872	5
VA90	624	0	624	0	112	512	17
AZ92	2,369	390	1,979	16	255	1,934	12
CO92	2,912	1,090	1,822	37	305	1,499	16
CT92	1,808	634	1,174	35	199	864	16
FL92	591	75	516	12	42	382	8
GA92	994	288	706	28	128	670	18
IA92	794	21	773	2	134	773	17
IL92	2,569	726	1,843	28	109	1,475	5
IN92	1,754	418	1,336	23	233	1,117	17
KS92	607	0	607	0	28	578	4
KY92	210	0	210	0	35	215	16
MD92	1,267	64	1,203	5	109	1,286	9
MO92	797	172	625	21	87	565	13
NC92	1,892	255	1,637	13	67	1,396	4
NV92	952	63	889	6	53	857	5
NY92	2,124	264	1,860	12	138	1,463	7
OH92	1,377	284	1,093	20	162	945	14
OK92	2,073	884	1,189	42	201	963	16
OR92	3,043	1,079	1,964	35	469	1,563	23
PA92	4,593	1,518	3,075	33	591	2,611	19
WA92	694	75	619	10	61	637	9
WI92	4,058	216	3,842	5	914	2,759	23
Total	89,427	17,439	71,988	888	10,767	59,946	604
Minimum	210	0	132	0	14	117	3
Maximum	5,202	1,518	4,520	50	972	3,371	26
Average	1,825	355	1,469	18	219	1,223	12

The level of dialogue fluctuates from race to race. Six races that had no articles falling into the instant dialogue category are 1988 Arizona (Degreen *vs.* DeConcini), 1988 Texas (Boutler *vs.* Bentsen), 1990 Oklahoma (Jones *vs.* Boron), 1990 Virginia (Warner *vs.* Spannaus), 1992 Kansas (Dole *vs.* O'Dell), and 1992 Kentucky (Williams *vs.* Ford). In

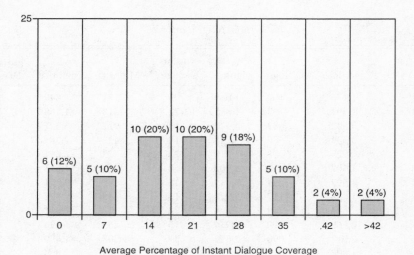

Figure 6.3   Distribution of instant dialogue across races.

contrast, five races – in order of largest proportion of dialogue, the 1988 Michigan (Dunn *vs.* Riegle), the 1990 Colorado (Brown *vs.* Heath), the 1992 Oklahoma (Nickles *vs.* Lewis), the 1992 Colorado (Considine *vs.* Campbell), the 1988 Washington (Gorton *vs.* Lowry) – had levels of instant dialogue greater than 36 percent. Offhand, there seems to be some relationship between the absolute level of content and the proportion of instant dialogue. This relationship is assessed in the next chapter. The overall distribution of instant dialogue appears in Figure 6.3.

As one can see, the typical range of instant dialogue proportions appears to be between 7 and 29 percent (34 races) with six and nine races falling below and above that range, respectively.

A similar pattern emerges with sustained dialogue. In absolute terms, the level is not high. Of the 71,988 lines that did not feature instant dialogue, 10,767 were coded as representing the minority side, leaving 59,946 representing majority positions on each dimension. Thus, minority views found expression in only 18 percent of the lines. Again, statistics for each race are presented in Table 6.6. The level of sustained dialogue also fluctuates from race to race. One race, the 1990 New Jersey (Whitman *vs.* Bradley), had only three percent. Yet, in three races more than 22 percent of the coverage lines were given over to minority-held views – the 1988 Washington (Gorton *vs.* Lowry), the 1992 Oregon (Packwood *vs.* AuCoin), the 1992 Wisconsin (Kasten *vs.* Feingold). The

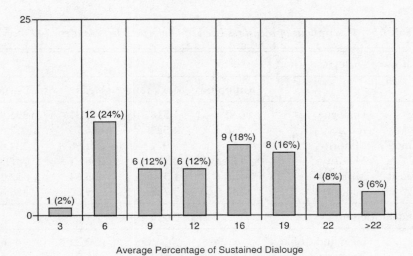

Figure 6.4   Distribution of sustained dialogue across races.

overall distribution of sustained dialogue appears in Figure 6.4. The typical range of sustained dialogue appears to be between six and 22 percent with all but the four aforementioned races falling in this range. Further analysis of these data, including an examination of dialogue by dimension, is saved for the next chapter.

Table 6.7 summarizes all the indicators produced for these analyses of the forty-nine races. Beginning with instant dialogue, some races feature no lines while the maximum is 1,518 lines. The average number of lines of instant dialogue is 363 with a standard deviation of 337. The number of lines in which candidates ignore each other within the same article works out to a minimum of 132 and a maximum of 4,520, so that the average number of within article ignoring lines is 1,487 with a standard deviation of 1,018. For sustained dialogue, the smallest amount of minority-held view discussion in a given race is fourteen lines while that indicator reaches its largest value at 972 lines with an average of 222 lines and a standard deviation of 234 lines. In contrast the amount of majority coverage ranges from 117 to 3,371 lines with an average of 1,238 lines and a standard deviation of 788 lines.

To produce a single overall measure of dialogue I combine the indicators for instant and sustained dialogue. They were combined arithmetically by splitting the level of instant dialogue in half and adding each half to the level of discussion of minority- and majority-held

Table 6.7   *Descriptions of Measures Used in Dialogue Effects Analysis (49 races)*

Indicators of Dialogue		Minimum	Maximum	Mean	Std. Deviation
Instant	Dialogue	0	1,518	363.31	336.91
	Ignore	132	4,520	1,486.75	1,017.69
Sustained	Minority	14	972	221.98	234.49
	Majority	117	3,371	1,238.21	787.51
Composite	Minority	28	1,350	403.64	352.35
	Majority	185.5	3,748	1,419.86	886.62
Dependent Measures					
	Likes and dislikes	.96	3.56	2.22	.65
	Recognize candidates	29.8	100	78.21	19.51
	Partisan defection	7.1	42.6	24.43	9.28
	Recall candidates	1.3	48.9	21.92	13.47
Control Variables					
	Presidential year	0	1	.71	.46
	Southern state	0	1	.21	.41
	Electoral margin	.8	66	17.33	14.34

views. This creates two new measures; first, there is a composite measure of minority-held views, which ranges from twenty-eight lines in the race with the lowest absolute level of dialogue to 1,350 lines in the race with the most. This composite measure of dialogue averages 404 lines with a standard deviation of 352 lines. Second there is a composite measure of majority-held views. Overall, they are discussed for at least 185 lines and at most 3,748 lines in each race with an average of 1,411 lines and a standard deviation of 886 lines. (The lower portion of Table 6.7 will be taken up in the next section.) This method can be justified by the following observation. Instant dialogue charts the level of engagement within each article. Thus, instant dialogue is composed of discussion of minority- as well as majority-held views. The sustained measure taps the campaign's level of dialogue apart from that inside of articles. Thus, to produce the composite measure the instant dialogue must be apportioned into the two sustained measures and the split is equal in order to work against the no dialogue prediction.

Table 6.8   *Correlations Across Indicators of Dialogue (49 races)*

		Instant Dialogue	Ignore	Sustained		Composite	
				Minority	Majority	Minority	Majority
Instant	Dialogue	—					
	Ignore	.53	—				
Sustained	Minority	.52	.92	—			
	Majority	.53	.98	.86	—		
Composite	Minority	.82	.86	.91	.82	—	
	Majority	.65	.97	.86	.99	.88	—

It is useful to examine the relationships between these six measures in order to prepare for the analysis of dialogue's effects. Table 6.8 presents the correlations among all six counts involved in this analysis of dialogue – lines of instant dialogue, lines where candidates ignored each other in the same article, lines of discussion of minority views and majority views in the campaign, and the two composite measures. These correlations range between .52, the correlation between the level of instant dialogue and the level of overall discussion of minority views and .98, the correlation between within article ignoring and its component, the level of overall discussion of majority views. The composite measures are also highly correlated with their components. These relationships range in strength from a correlation of .65 between the level of overall discussion of majority held views and the level of instant dialogue to .99, the correlation between the overall level of discussion of majority views and the level of sustained discussion of majority views. Discussion of minority and majority views is correlated in the sustained as well as the composite measures, at .86 and .88, respectively.

THE EFFECTS OF DIALOGUE

With these measures in hand, we can digress and examine dialogue's effects. Chapter two presented a normative argument – linking the quality of public discourse to democratic governance – that spelled out some beneficial consequences of dialogue. The data on senate campaigns provide an opportunity to conduct an empirical test on some of these propositions. In general, good public discourse is thought to increase citizens' feelings of public efficacy, their political knowledge, and the depth of their political decisions. All of these effects can be assessed using the appropriate data, however, the data I will use in this section are less than perfect. The data were collected as part of the National Election Studies Senate Election Study, which was a set of relatively short surveys designed to assess voting behavior in senate elections across the fifty states. As a result of its length, the measures of voting quality are not as plentiful as one might hope. With that said, this analysis does contribute to our belief in dialogue's beneficial effects.

The SES data used here were collected after each of the forty-nine elections that are part of my study. A mostly representative sample of roughly fifty voters were asked questions, four of which can be used as indicators of what can be called the quality of voting. In each case the dependent measure of dialogue's beneficial effect is the average response of these fifty voters. In addition, three control variables are used in an attempt to statistically account for rival explanations. Descriptions of all the indicators are presented in the lower two panels of Table 6.7. I will discuss the dependent measures first and leave discussion of the control variables until later.

The first indicator, called likes and dislikes, codes the number of answers the average respondent gave to a standard survey question asking what they like or dislike about a particular candidate. For every mention for either candidate, respondents were awarded one point; thus, this measure is the total number of points the average respondent received in each race. Most researchers (see Westlye 1991) argue that the more respondents say in answer to this question, the better, given that more answers are indicative of having more political information. In my forty-nine races the lowest average number of mentions was .96 while the highest was 3.56 mentions, meaning the typical person mentioned one to three and a half things for both candidates. The average number of mentions was 2.22 with a standard deviation of .65 mentions.

Voters are also assumed to be better informed when they vote against their partisan attachments. As discussed in chapter three, partisanship is the cue that most often determines voting behavior. As it is a very simple cue that is based on an "emotional attachment," voting against one's partisanship signals that the voter is using a more complex strategy. In short, the level of partisan defection is another indicator of the quality of a race, where more defection is generally better. The measure I employ below is constructed from the respondent's reports concerning their vote and their self-reported partisanship. It is coded one if they defect by voting for a candidate with a different partisanship and zero otherwise. In these races the lowest level of partisan defection was 7.1 percent while the highest was about 43 percent, meaning that almost half the voters voted against their emotional tie to a party. The average defection rate was about 24 percent with a standard deviation of 9.3 percent.

The third measure, recognition, involves the respondents being able to correctly identify the candidates' names. This indicator charts the percentage of respondents who were able to correctly identify the candidates from a list that was read to them. More recognition equates to more knowledge and, consequently, better votes. In the worst race, only 29.8 percent recognized one candidate while in the best all the respondents, 100 percent, did so. The average recognition rate was 78.2 with a standard deviation of 19.5. The final measure, recall, indicates the percentage of respondents that were able to correctly name the two major party candidates participating in a race.

In addition, the respondents also had to correctly match each candidate to their parties. This more stringent test of voter knowledge produced worse average results because it is easier to recognize someone's name than to recall it. At best, slightly less than half, 48.9 percent, of voters, accurately recalled both candidates and their parties while, at worst, slightly over one percent of the voters were able to do so. On average 22 percent of the respondents demonstrated correct recall with a standard deviation of 13.5 percent.

RESULTS

Regression is the quickest way to estimate the effect of different kinds of discourse on the quality of voting. The four indicators of voting quality are those just mentioned in the above discussion – number of likes and dislikes as well as the rates of partisan defection, recognition, and recall. In the first set of specifications I will examine, the regression model compares the lines of dialogue or discussion of minority-held views to lines without dialogue or discussion of majority-held views. In this way, the impacts of different kinds of campaign speech can be assessed while indirectly controlling for the total amount of speech. A second set of similar specifications will produce the same estimates of effects for the composite measure as well as another set with some relatively standard controls for alternative hypotheses.

Because I only have data on forty-nine cases and because there already is a certain amount of correlation within the measures of

Table 6.9   *The Effects of Instant and Sustained Dialogue (49 races)*

		Likes and Dislikes		Recognize Candidates	
Instant	Dialogue	.06**	2.14**		
	Ignore	.02**	.59**		
Sustained	Minority		.07		3.32*
	Majority		.02		.30
	Constant	1.69	1.79	61.62	67.16
	Adj. R-sq.	.28	.21	.32	.22
		Partisan Defection		Recall Candidates	
Instant	Dialogue	−.77*		1.67**	
	Ignore	−.02		.57**	
Sustained	Minority		−.82		2.97**
	Majority		.03		.30
	Constant	27.46	25.94	7.30	11.59
	Adj. R-sq.	.04	.01	.53	.43

Note: All content measures are in hundreds of lines. Asterisks indicate levels of statistical significance: ***$p < .01$; **$p < .05$; *$p < .1$.

campaign speech, these specifications seem to be optimal. They produce direct estimates of increases in vote quality due to increasing the number of lines of that discourse type. In all cases, the lines of discourse are divided by one hundred to make the parameter estimates one hundred times greater, so that each estimate represents the impact of a hundred lines of discourse. This transformation makes the estimates easier to read and to discuss, but has no substantive implications for the results.

The initial regression estimates for each of the four variables of interest are presented in the panels of Table 6.9. Two specifications are estimated for each measure. In each case, the specification in the first column pits the level of instant dialogue against the amount of within article ignoring while the second column contrasts the level of discussion of minority views against the level of majority view discussion. The results for likes and dislikes appear in the upper left-hand panel. Every hundred lines of instant dialogue produce another .06 mentions; on the other hand, every hundred lines of within article ignoring discourse produce an increase of only .02 mentions. Both of these estimates are statistically significant at the .05 level, and the regression itself has an r^2 value of .28, indicating that the variation in campaign speech type explains almost a third of the variance in likes and dislikes mentioned. So dialogue produces about three times as much of an increase as does the equivalent discourse absent dialogue. A similar pattern appears for sustained dialogue, the estimate for minority-held views is over three times greater than that of the majority; these results, however, are not statistically significant.

Turning to the lower left-hand panel of Table 6.9, we can examine the results for partisan defection. The impacts are not as statistically significant; nevertheless, the magnitude of the estimates suggest that dialogue and its companion, discussion of majority-held views, exert beneficial effects on the electorate. In both cases the effect on reducing partisan voting is substantially greater with the qualitatively better speech. While a hundred lines of instant dialogue decreased the inferior kind of voting by almost .8, which is statistically significant at the .1 level, its opposite – ignoring lines within articles – had a negligible impact. The same holds for the sustained measures, as well. Discussion of minority views had a large but statistically insignificant impact, and the impact of majority view discussion was negligible.

The results concerning recall and recognition are stronger. In the upper right-hand panel of Table 6.9, a hundred lines of instant dialogue produced an average increase of two percent in the recognition rate per race. Meanwhile, a hundred lines in which the candidates ignored each other only produced an increase of .6 percent. Again the effect of dialogue is over three times greater, and both of these estimates are significant at the .05 level. An even greater disparity exists for the sustained measures. A hundred lines of minority discussion produces an increase of over three percent, significant at the .1 level, but the same majority discussion produces an increase that does not statistically differ from zero.

Recall follows the same pattern though the effects are of smaller magnitude because recall is more stringent test of knowledge. The estimates are shown in the lower right-hand panel of Table 6.9. A hundred lines of dialogue increase the percentage of respondents recalling both candidates and their party in the race by one-and-a-half percent; the same amount of discussion where candidates ignore each other leads to half a percent increase. Again these estimates are significant at the .05 level. The results for sustained discussion are even more dramatic for recall. A hundred lines of minority view discussion are worth an almost 3 percent increase in recall, which is also significant at the .05 level. The same amount of discussion of majority views again is not statistically different from zero.

It may be argued that these tests do not adequately consider some alternative hypotheses, so I estimated all these models a second time using the composite measure of dialogue while statistically controlling for three rival explanations. It should be noted that the statistical comparisons already contain an implicit control for the amount of campaign discussion, which some take to be the intensity of the race. The results with respect to the effects of dialogue are almost identical. The three rival explanations for voting quality include being in a presidential electoral cycle (called presidential year), being in a southern state, and the margin of the winning candidate's victory. Descriptive statistics for these three items are presented in the lower panel of Table 6.7. The first two are dummy variables that are coded one for 1988 and 1992 and zero for 1990, and one for races that happened in the south and zero otherwise. The idea supporting this indicator is that during presidential years voting quality is either chronically higher or lower, respectively. Margin is used as another measure of intensity, with higher numbers indicating that the race is more hard fought (see Westlye 1991). It is expressed as a percentage and ranges from .8 in the closest race to 66 in the most lopsided. The average electoral gap was around 17 percent with a standard deviation of 14.3 percent.

The new regression estimates appear in the panels of Table 6.10. Again, two specifications are estimated for each measure. In each case, the specification in the first column pits the composite measure of minority discussion against the composite measure of majority discussion while the second column presents the same contrast with the three control variables. The results for likes and dislikes appear in the upper left-hand panel. Here, every hundred lines of minority discussion produce another .08 mentions, which is statistically significant at the .05 level, though every hundred lines of majority discussion produce an increase of only .01 mentions. With the controls, the results become slightly weaker. The statistical significance moves down to the .1 level for the first coefficient because the indicator for presidential year is highly significant.

The other three indicators of voting quality follow the same pattern. In all three of these cases minority discussion has a stronger effect than majority discussion. Only with recognition, the upper right-hand panel of Table 6.10, do the controls markedly change the level of statistical significance of this effect. In this instance the effect of minority discussion

Table 6.10   The Effects of Composite Dialogue Measures with Controls
(49 races)

		Likes and Dislikes		Recognize Candidates	
Composite	Minority	.08**	.08*	3.43**	1.42
	Majority	.01	.00	−.08	.23
Presidential year			−.37**		3.86
Southern state			−.16		−6.88*
Electoral margin			−.01		−.72
	Constant	1.74	2.20	65.47	65.40
	Adj. R-sq.	.28	.31	.51	.55
		Partisan Defection		Recall Candidates	
Composite	Minority	−1.10*	−.43	2.76**	2.11**
	Majority	.18	.14	.01	.13
Presidential year			.66		−.12
Southern state			−1.33		−2.77
Electoral margin			.32**		−.25**
	Constant	26.27	18.41	10.01	10.52
	Adj. R-sq.	.04	.20	.55	.58

Note: All content measures are in hundreds of lines. Asterisks indicate levels of statistical significance: ***$p < .01$; **$p < .05$; *$p < .1$.

is not significant with controls. This change is due to chronically lower recognition rates in southern states and not due to presidential year or electoral margin. A similar change takes place with partisan defection, in the lower left-hand panel of Table 6.10. The effect of the composite minority discussion indicator is not large to begin with and it falls with the controls, as the effect of electoral margin in this case is significant. Electoral margin is also significant in the case of recall, however, it does not change the significance of minority discussion, which is highly significant in both columns of the lower right hand panel.

SUMMARY

The analyses of the content data in this chapter confirm some important points and lay the groundwork for an understanding of the dynamics of dialogue in the next chapter. In the first place, it confirms our earlier intuitions and predictions concerning the amount of dialogue. By any measure the amount of dialogue observed in these campaigns is low, generally falling between 10 and 15 percent. On the other hand, the dialogue that appears is advantageous from the voters' perspective. The level of dialogue correlates well with the amount of knowledge that the voters have in specific races. In contrast, the campaign speech that does not feature dialogue bears less relationship to the level of voter knowledge. In sum, these rare instances of dialogue are precious and need to be examined more closely. The next chapter takes up this task, completing the analyses of these senate elections.

CHAPTER 7

Explaining and Predicting the Occurrence
of Dialogue

The data on Senate campaign content examined in the previous chapter indicates that some dialogue does indeed take place. These instances of dialogue make it possible to test ideas as to when dialogue will occur. In particular, these relatively rare instances of dialogue can be used to build a statistical model, which explains dialogue's occurrence. This analysis will require additional data, specifically information on the candidates' positions and other background factors. By developing this explanation, we will be able to generate predictions as to when to expect dialogue. Thus, this final analysis should complete our understanding of the dynamics surrounding campaign dialogue.

I will begin with a reexamination of the game-theoretic model that was originally presented in chapter three. This reexamination will concentrate on developing hypotheses to explain dialogue's appearances. I will develop hypotheses related to the newspaper's editorial policies, characteristics of dimensions and the candidates' positions (among others) that will predict and explain the occurrence of dialogue. The new data necessary to test these hypotheses will be introduced and the appropriate tests conducted. By the end of this chapter, we will have an understanding derived from the model as to when circumstances will lead to more substantive electoral campaigns.

SUMMARY OF THE MODEL

The concept of dialogue served as this investigation's point of departure. I framed the decision to dialogue or not as a strategic choice, made in light of the candidates' expectations as to what responding to or ignoring a particular campaign theme would do to their electoral prospects. Using the mathematical machinery of game theory, in chapter three I developed a formal model that identified the forces acting on candidates' choices over what themes to discuss in their campaign message. In so doing, the model made and supported a prediction as to why dialogue does not occur. As we shall see, the model can also highlight some circumstances that may bring about dialogue, which I will discuss and develop as hypotheses in the following section.

To review briefly, the model synthesizes the literature on voting behavior, political communication, and candidate strategy. In the company of other political behavior researchers (Zaller 1992; Kinder and Sanders 1997), it begins with the claim that there are an infinite number of potential considerations that may affect an individual's vote. These considerations correspond to topics the candidates can choose to discuss in the campaign. When candidates discuss a topic, they raise the importance or salience of that topic in the voters' minds, so voters weigh that consideration more heavily in casting their ballots. This critical empirical premise concerning campaign communication is known as the priming effect (Iyengar and Kinder 1987; Krosnick and Kinder 1990). Rational candidates want to prime the topics they believe will enhance their electoral prospects.

The model resolved two questions. First, what themes should candidates discuss? The candidates' allocation strategies depend on the relative positions of the candidates. Following Black's (1958) and others median voter logic, a candidate does best in terms of increasing expected vote by choosing to talk about those themes on which he or she is relatively closer to the median voter's expected position. Second, why do candidates avoid dialogue? Assuming their positions differ, only one candidate is advantaged on any theme. The advantaged candidate should and will discuss that theme because the message will increase the weight voters attach to that issue and therefore increase that candidate's advantage. Because voters' weights can only increase as a result of campaign discussion, the advantage of the advantaged candidate will also increase if the other candidate responds by talking about that same theme. Thus, candidates will spend all their resources discussing themes where they are advantaged and none on themes where they are disadvantaged. This result rules out the possibility for dialogue among strictly rational candidates.

EXPLAINING DIALOGUE'S OCCURRENCE

From this understanding of the dynamics of dialogue, some hypotheses concerning dialogue's appearance can be developed. In particular, further examination of the model's underlying assumptions provides clues as to when dialogue is likely to occur. First, there are factors that have been left out of the basic model. For example, the presence of dialogue in newspaper coverage of campaigns may be the result of newspapers' editorial policies. The model avoids dealing with the vagaries of the journalistic process, but we may need to recognize the effects of these choices to understand the appearance of dialogue in actual campaign coverage. Second, the no dialogue result is predicated on a specific logic linking the assumptions to the conclusions. If, in part, the assumptions do not apply to the real world, we might see dialogue. For instance, special contextual circumstances may limit the communications options available to candidates in ways absent from the general case the model describes. This dialogue is explainable within the scope of the model and may be valuable in terms of enhancing campaign discourse. For example, when historical and other circumstances force campaigners to discuss only one issue or a cluster of closely correlated issues, as in so-called critical elections, a dialogue necessarily occurs. Of course, as the model holds, this kind of dialogue hurts the disadvantaged candidate's chances.

In a similar vein, the model is built on the assumption that candidates are rational only in that they discuss dimensions on which they are advantaged. Irrational candidates, who violate this assumption, are more likely to produce dialogue. Candidates who hold extreme positions, for instance, are in a sense behaving irrationally. They are not subject to the model's logical imperatives and may dialogue in their campaigns. Finally, the candidates may create a pseudodialogue, which I call reframing. Candidates can subtly shift dimensions, attempting to reframe an opponent's thematic initiative. In my view, dialogue of this kind is the best that can be expected in the present political regime. The choice to reframe a discussion lies somewhere along the discourse continuum in between the options of responding or ignoring. It is much more difficult to study as it not as amenable to a clear experimental manipulation or empirical observation; however, it does represent an avenue for increasing the quality of discourse. Because it is not directly studied, consideration of this topic is held for the concluding chapter.

Taken together, these situations constitute the areas in which dialogue is likeliest to occur. I will discuss them as I develop and test concrete hypotheses for the Senate data. Before that, I discuss the modifications and additions to the Senate campaign content dataset necessary to test these and related hypotheses.

MEETING THE DATA REQUIREMENTS

Moving from a description of the overall level of dialogue to a scientific study of when dialogue occurs calls for more precise data about the instances of dialogue themselves. Thus far in the Senate study, I have examined the occurrence of dialogue using mainly the Senate race as the unit of analysis. From now on I will take every opportunity for dialogue as the unit of analysis, creating a much larger set of data that will allow subsequent examinations to be better tuned. For example, instead of knowing that the North Carolina race featured more dialogue than other races, we shall explore on what dimensions dialogue in that particular race occurred and compare those instances to all other points at which dialogue was possible.

Given that we have forty-nine races with thirty-two dimensions each, there are 1,568 potential instances of dialogue in the data. Note, of these, there are 788 opportunities (about half) where no campaign discussion occurred at all. Arranging the data in this fashion makes it possible to reexamine the three measures of dialogue introduced in the last chapter – instant, sustained, and composite – in a more informative way by converting them to percentage measures. Thus, instead of a dichotomous measure which indicates whether dialogue appears or it doesn't, we can quantify the relative amount of dialogue that occurs at every opportunity. In this process, for the instant dialogue indicator, the total number of lines of discussion divides the total lines of instant dialogue. The resulting measure runs from zero, meaning no dialogue, to 100 percent, with the average percentage roughly equal to 7.1. At the minimum, there are 1,358 instances where no dialogue occurs and only thirty-nine instances with 100 percent instant dialogue.

For the measure of sustained dialogue, the minimum is zero and the maximum is 50 percent with the average at 4.4 percent. Here 1,303 instances are at the zero level and three at the maximum. Finally, the composite measure also runs between zero and 50 but with an average of 7.3 percent. Here, there are 1,192 cases at the minimum (76 percent) and forty-two at the maximum. The correlations between these three measures of dialogue are as reported in the last chapter. To review, the level of instant dialogue is correlated with the level of sustained dialogue at .14. Both of these measures are correlated with the composite measure at around .74.

With these dependent measures in hand, I can describe some of the other data that will be employed in the analysis of these instances. Most important, given the dictates of the model, I constructed a data set that charted the candidates' positions. I also procured other background data relevant to the study on each of the Senate races. Here I discuss the candidate positions data and discuss the rest of the background data as it is used.

In my model of campaigns in mass elections the candidates' positions play a leading role, as they are the only exogenous factor. This fact made it vital to collect this information for use in the analysis of the occurrence of dialogue. This collection was based on the premise from chapter three that the candidates' strengths and weaknesses are well known to political insiders. To gather the data, two small teams of researchers combed all the sources available to political experts at the time of the election except for the newspaper coverage used in the content analysis. These sources included the *Almanac of American Politics, Congressional Quarterly, Politics in America, Facts On File, Biographical Directory of the U.S. Congress, Campaigns and Elections Magazine, Cook Political Report*, and *Roll Call Magazine*.

For each dimension, each team rated each candidate. Then the two ratings were reconciled on a ten-point scale where one is the most liberal and ten is the most conservative. Candidates who were perfectly moderate received a 5.5. This scoring produced a total of 3,136 ratings. On the whole, the Republican candidates had a mean position of 7.5 with a standard deviation of 1.9 points while the Democratic candidates had a mean position of 3.4 also with a standard deviation of 1.9 points. With these indicators as well as some more background information collected from the same sources, the analysis of patterns in the appearance of dialogue can begin.

All the ratings were also graded according to the amount of information behind each. Three levels were used, where three represents the most material and one the least. All the analysis reported below were conducted twice. The first run employed all the data from all the dimensions while the second included only those with the most material, that is those in category three. As no significant difference appeared between these two analyses, only the results for the entire data are reported.

EDITORIAL POLICY'S INFLUENCE ON DIALOGUE'S APPEARANCE

To embark on a systematic study of the factors responsible for the appearance of dialogue, we must first consider an alternative that has been avoided to this point. There is a long tradition of media studies that pedestals the role of editors and other gatekeepers in deciding what is news (Epstein 1973; Sigal 1973; Tuchman 1978; Gans 1979). To carry these arguments another step, one might infer that the actions of these players govern the appearance of dialogue. While my formal model ignores this possibility, it merits investigation nonetheless. In this section, I use the data at hand to investigate the effects of what I will call editorial policy on the presence or absence of substantive campaign coverage, that is, dialogue. First, I document the relationship observed in the previous chapter that more coverage seems to lead to a greater proportion of dialogue. Then, I look at the level of dialogue in each paper. Because the number of observations per paper are limited to one or two races, I also use region as a proxy for editorial policy on the assumption that readers, and therefore editors, in the same parts of the country have more similar tastes. Some other potential but untestable editorial effects are left for discussion in the final chapter.

Beginning with a relationship suggested by Table 6.6, it seems that more coverage leads to a greater percentage of dialogue. Because the amount of coverage is, at least in part, a matter of editorial policy this is an appropriate time to assess this notion. Using ordinary regression to test this relationship verifies the amount of coverage is indeed associated with the level of dialogue. For instant dialogue, every hundred lines of coverage produce an increase of 4.6 percent in the amount observed. This estimate has a standard error of .42, making the coefficient significant at the .01 level. This means that there is only one chance in a hundred that this relationship is due to chance. Likewise, every hundred lines of coverage produces an increase of 4 percent in the level of sustained dialogue. This estimate has a standard error of .21, which also makes it significant at the .01 level. Increases in the level of coverage, thus dramatically increase the likelihood of observing dialogue in a given unit of coverage.

The idea that editorial policy affects the amount of substance in coverage also motivates a closer look at dialogue's appearance in each paper. With only forty-nine races included in this sample, taking the newspaper as unit of analysis is problematic because there are only one or two observations for each case. However, it is instructive to at least look at the differences across papers. Table 7.1 lists all the papers and the average percentage of instant and sustained dialogue that appeared in the associated races. The differences across papers are quite striking, even if, as we should, we limit examination to those papers with two

Table 7.1 *Analyses of Editorial Effects: Substantive Coverage by Paper (sorted)*

Instant Dialogue			Sustained Dialogue		
Newspaper	Races	Percent	Newspaper	Races	Percent
Mountain News	90, 92	14.79	*Inquirer*	92	12.23
Chicago Tribune	90, 92	13.6	*World-Herald*	88, 90	10.4
Oregonian	90, 92	12.59	*Miami Journal*	92	9.42
Courant	92	12.52	*Observer*	90, 92	7.44
Star Tribune	88, 90	11.42	*Star Tribune*	88, 90	6.69
Boston Globe	88, 90	10.43	*Boston Globe*	88, 90	6.31
Post-Dispatch	88, 92	8.85	*AZ Republic*	88, 92	5.9
LA Times	88	8.66	*Courier-Journal*	90, 92	5.63
Tribune/World	90, 92	8.29	*Register*	92	5.61
Dispatch	88, 92	8.02	*Oregonian*	90, 92	5.24
Observer	90, 92	7.83	*Chicago Tribune*	90, 92	4.68
New York Times	88, 92	7.32	*Courant*	92	4.61
Free Press	88, 90	6.85	*Tribune/World*	90, 92	4.35
M. Journal	92	6.81	*Seattle Times*	88, 92	4.11
I. News	90, 92	6.57	*SP Times*	88, 92	3.8
World-Herald	90	6.56	*LV Review*	92	3.76
Courier-Journal	90, 92	6.44	*Mountain News*	90, 92	3.54
Wichita Eagle	90	5.91	*I. News*	90, 92	3.26
Inquirer	92	5.01	*NY Times*	88, 92	2.95
NJ Record	88, 90	4.75	*ATL Constitution*	92	2.89
Seattle Times	88, 92	4.7	*Free Press*	88, 90	2.7
Constitution	92	4.5	*Morning News*	88, 90	2.59
Republic	88, 92	3.8	*NJ Record*	88, 90	2.27
SP Times	88, 92	3.7	*Baltimore Sun*	92	2.16
LV Review	92	3.59	*Dispatch*	88, 92	2.02
Register	92	3.12	*News Leader*	90	1.95
Baltimore Sun	92	2.28	*LA Times*	88	1.62
Morning News	88, 90	1.21	*Post-Dispatch*	88, 92	1.27
News Leader	90	0	*Wichita Eagle*	90	1.1
Kansas City Star	92	0	*Kansas City Star*	92	.89

races. For the eighteen papers with two races, the level of instant dialogue ranges from a high of 14.8 percent in the case of the *Rocky Mountain News* to a low of 1.2 percent in the case of the *Dallas Morning News*. A smaller spread is observed for the percentage of sustained dialogue. It ranges from a high of 7.4 percent for the *Charlotte Observer* to a low of 1.3 percent for the *St. Louis Dispatch*. The limited number of observations demands that we interpret these results cautiously, but, at the least, this spread suggests that there are idiosyncratic factors that govern the appearance of dialogue at each paper. At the same time, the difference in the ranges of results from instant dialogue to sustained dialogue suggests that editorial policy plays a larger role where instant dialogue is concerned.

Given these effects it is important to take two more steps. First, the impact of editorial policy should be quantified, and second, a measure of editorial policy should be incorporated as a control in further analyses of dialogue's appearance. I will rely on using region of the country as a proxy measure to fulfill these requirements. The argument for using region should assume that all editors have a perception of what the readers demand in the form of campaign coverage. Readers who live closer to each other are more likely to have similar preferences than those who live farther away. Therefore editors in the same region of the country should be more likely to follow the same editorial policies than editors in different regions.

Using the eight-region breakdown developed by the National Election Studies, we can classify each paper according to each geographical location. This produces an average of six observations per case. While still not a lot, this grouping produces some statistical leverage on the problem at hand. Table 7.2 reports the breakdown of papers into regions and lists the amount of instant and sustained dialogue in each. The range of instant dialogue runs from a high of 11 percent in New England to a low of about 4 percent in the South with most regions falling between 6 and 8 percent. The range is not quite so broad in the case of sustained dialogue. It runs from a high of 6 in New England to a low of about 4 in the East Central area. In the case of instant dialogue these differences are significant at the .01 level while for sustained dialogue they are not statistically significant. This analysis suggests that editorial policy causes a substantive difference at least in the case of instant dialogue. In addition, further analysis of dialogue will include variables to control for the race's presence in the south as well as in New England.

VIOLATIONS OF ASSUMPTIONS
CONCERNING DIMENSIONS

The development of any rational choice model begins with a set of assumptions from which the model springs. One of the major assump-

Table 7.2   *Analysis of Editorial Effects: Substantive Coverage by Region*

Region	Newspapers	Dialogue	
		Instant Percent	Sustained Percent
Pacific	Los Angeles Times	8.65	4.06
	Portland Oregonian		
	Seattle Times		
Mountain	Arizona Republic	8.15	4.53
	Las Vegas Review-Journal		
	Rocky Mountain News		
South	Atlanta Constitution	3.75	4.06
	Charlotte Observer		
	Dallas Morning News		
	Richmond News Leader		
	St. Petersburg Times		
Border	Baltimore Sun	6.35	4.42
	Courier-Journal		
	Tulsa Tribune/World		
New England	Boston Globe	11.13	5.75
	Hartford Courant		
Mid-Atlantic	New Jersey Record	5.83	4.53
	New York Times		
	Philadelphia Inquirer		
East Central	Chicago Tribune	8.55	3.86
	Columbus Dispatch		
	Detroit Free Press		
	Indianapolis News		
	Milwaukee Journal		
West Central	Des Moines Register	6.98	4.91
	Kansas City Star		
	Minneapolis Star Tribune		
	Omaha World-Herald		
	St Louis Post-Dispatch		
	Wichita Eagle		

tions I have made is that dimensions are analytically indistinguishable. I also assume that an infinite number or dimensions are potentially available for discussion. But these assumptions may not be fully accurate in the real world of campaign discourse. Political scientists, for example, have done a great deal of work that separates some discussion topics from others. In this section I apply the logics proposed by various researchers to see if certain types of dimensions may be more likely to feature dialogue. In preparation for the final statistical model, we shall examine the effects of Petrocik's (1996) idea of issue ownership and Stokes's (1966) notion of consensual issues. Finally, I examine instances where only a limited number of dimensions are available for discussion, as in so-called critical elections.

To begin analysis of dimensional characteristics, let's examine the level of dialogue observed on each. Table 7.3 presents two lists of all thirty-two dimensions sorted according to the overall amount of instant and sustained dialogue that appeared. There is wide variation across dimensions. Instant dialogue runs from a high of 38 percent in the case of health to a low of nothing in the case of five dimensions (immigration, gridlock, liberal, religion, and biography). There is a smaller but similar spread for sustained dialogue. It runs from 24 percent for farms and health to zero in the case of immigration and personality. It also appears that the rank order is nearly the same across the two measures of dialogue. To examine this variation more closely, we will turn to the political science literature on issues and see whether these arguments help to explain this variation in the presence of dialogue.

ISSUE OWNERSHIP

Petrocik (1996) puts forward one argument as to why some issues may be different than others. Under the heading of "issue ownership," Petrocik argues that there are chronic differences in the way the public sees the Republican and Democratic parties. These stereotypes give rise to differing perceptions concerning each party's competence in handling certain issues. For example, stereotypes about the Republican Party lead the public to believe that they will do a better job handling the dimension of defense. Likewise, these same stereotypes lead people to believe that the Democrats will do a better job with welfare. This logic also carries implications for how the candidates campaign. As reported in chapter one, Petrocik (1996) argues that because of these long-term biases candidates will do best speaking only about issues they own and ignoring the rest.

The left-hand column of Table 7.4 documents this effect in the Senate campaign content data. Here, the thirty-two dimensions are sorted according to the percentage of the candidate material that came from the Democratic candidate. As can be seen there is a divergence, just as

Table 7.3   *Level of Dialogue by Dimension (sorted)*

Instant Dialogue				Sustained Dialogue			
Dimension	Dial.	Ignore	Percent	Dimension	Majority	Minority	Percent
HEALTH	1,900	3,071	38	FARMS	621	199	24
FARMS	456	819	35	HEALTH	2,541	839	24
ECON	2,260	4,110	35	ABORT	1,601	502	23
ABORT	1,065	2,099	33	BIO	621	172	21
TRADE	554	1,286	30	ECON	3,307	831	20
FORPOL	763	2,050	27	TAX	4,083	970	19
ENVIRON	1,805	4,934	26	PERF	4,856	1,171	19
CRIME	1,067	3,334	24	CRIME	3,171	717	18
DEFEND	860	2,816	23	DEFEND	2,336	482	17
SPEND	944	3,637	20	TRADE	1,068	219	17
PACS	825	3,210	20	SPEND	3,367	673	16
TAX	970	4,127	19	CIVRTS	1,561	296	15
PERF	1,360	5,925	18	INTEG	2,901	521	15
SOCSEC	318	1,617	16	ENVIRON	4,436	748	14
INTEG	668	3,292	16	SOCSEC	1,486	251	14
CIVRTS	325	1,856	14	FORPOL	1,902	301	13
EDUC	253	1,873	11	WASH	1,662	256	13
WELF	131	1,121	10	SCANDAL	2,119	240	10
WASH	220	1,841	10	WOMEN	1,480	170	10
REGS	56	732	7	PORK	780	93	10
WOMEN	116	1,650	6	EDUC	1,763	191	9
PORK	57	872	6	RELIG	1,217	128	9
SCANDAL	126	2,360	5	COMP	612	66	9
FLIP	38	716	5	REGS	791	78	8
PERSON	28	470	5	LIB	2,449	196	7
COMP	16	678	2	PACS	3,039	235	7
CON	16	1,129	1	WELF	1,112	74	6
IMMIG	0	69	0	CON	1,118	81	6
GRID	0	755	0	FLIP	672	47	6
LIB	26	3,674	0	GRID	735	20	2
RELIG	0	1,288	0	IMMIG	69	0	0
BIO	0	735	0	PERSON	470	0	0
Total	17,223	68,146			59,946	10,767	
Minimum	0	69	0		69	0	0
Maximum	2,260	5,925	38		4,856	1,171	24
Average	538	2,129	14		1,873	336	12

Table 7.4   *Categorization of Dimensions by Party Ownership and Consensuality*

Owner	Dimension	Percent of Dem. Lines	Type	Dimension
Republicans	IMMIG	7	Consensual	BIO
	PERSON	8		FLIP
	LIB	12		GRID
	CRIME	31		INTEG
	COMP	33		PACS
	SPEND	33		PERF
				PERSON
Neither	FORPOL	35		PORK
Party	TAX	35		SCANDAL
	REGS	36		WASH
	PERF	38		
	DEFEND	39	Valenced	ABORT
	PORK	40		CIVRTS
	RELIG	40		COMP
	FARMS	45		CON
	PACS	46		CRIME
	HEALTH	48		DEFEND
	INTEG	50		ECON
	BIO	51		EDUC
	WASH	51		ENVIRON
	ABORT	53		FARMS
	CIVRTS	53		FORPOL
	SCANDAL	57		HEALTH
	ECON	58		IMMIG
	TRADE	62		LIB
	GRID	65		REGS
	FLIP	68		RELIG
	SOCSEC	72		SOCSEC
				SPEND
Democrats	WELF	75		TAX
	ENVIRON	79		TRADE
	WOMEN	81		WELF
	EDUC	82		WOMEN
	CON	85		

(N = 32 Dimensions)

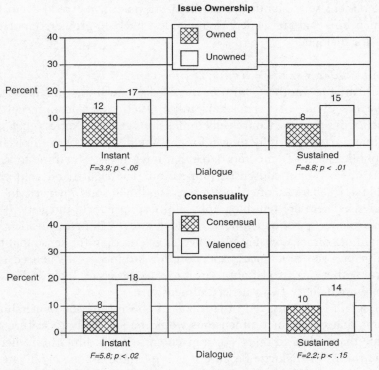

Figure 7.1 The impact of issue type on levels of dialogue (N = 32 dimensions).

Petrocik would predict. The Democrats do very little speaking about immigration and being a liberal while they instigate a great deal of discussion about welfare, women's issues, and the like. It seems probable that this impetus would affect the likelihood of observing dialogue on these dimensions, and indeed it does. As the upper panel in Figure 7.1 illustrates, there is much less dialogue on the eleven owned dimensions presented (listed in Table 7.4) as compared to the remaining, unowned, dimensions. The differences are not overly dramatic but they are statistically and substantively significant. Comparing the owned to unowned dimensions for instant dialogue we see almost twice as many lines (345 to 626) and an increase of five percent, from 12 to 17. This difference is significant at the .06 level. For sustained dialogue the effect is greater. The number of lines moves up from 224 to 387 and the percentage increase is 7, from 8 to 15 percent. The latter increase is significant at the .01 level. So, it would seem that dimensions that are owned are much less likely to provide opportunities for dialogue.

CONSENSUAL VERSUS VALENCE DIMENSIONS

Turning to another common way of distinguishing dimensions, we have the divide between what Stokes (1966) called consensual and valence dimensions. Consensual dimensions are more or less goals, and so they are not generally subject for partisan dispute. For example, both Republicans and Democrats agree that integrity is something to value; thus integrity is a consensual dimension. The right-hand column of Table 7.4 separates out the consensual dimensions involved in this analysis. There are ten: biography, flip-flop, gridlock, integrity, PACs, performance, personality, pork, scandal, and Washington insider. The remaining dimensions are identified as valenced, in the sense that they admit partisan differences. Abortion, for instance, is a valenced issue because there are two (if not more) sides to this issue. Table 7.4 lists the remaining twenty-two valenced dimensions.

Using a logic similar to that detailed above for issue ownership, it seems that consensual dimensions would be less likely to feature dialogue than valenced ones. For a given consensual dimension, there is little room for dialogue because it is impossible for the candidates to disagree by definition. The lower panel in Figure 7.1 shows the average level of instant and sustained dialogue for consensus and valence dimension. Again, there is a clear if not dramatic pattern. In terms of instant dialogue, there are only 303 lines on consensual dimension but 661 lines on valenced dimensions. This represents an increase of 10 percent, from 8 to 18. This increase is statistically significant at the .02 level. For sustained dialogue a similar but smaller increase appears. There are 256 lines on consensual dimensions and 378, on average for valenced ones. This is an increase of 4 percent from 10 to 14. The difference for sustained dialogue approaches statistical significance – the p-level is .15. Thus, we observe that consensual dimensions are less likely to provide opportunities for dialogue.

CRITICAL ELECTIONS

Assumptions about the political environment also point the way toward circumstances leading to dialogue. The model assumes that candidates will have an infinite number of dimensions to choose from when they construct their message. This is not always the case. Sometimes exogenous factors work to limit their choice, and force candidates to dialogue. The most obvious of these circumstances accompanies so-called critical elections and political events.

Critical elections occur when conflicting political tides emerge from the background environment into the light of an election (Burnham 1970). These elections turn on a singular great issue or a cluster of closely correlated issues. Circumstance thus shrinks the number of dimensions available for discussion to one and candidates are limited to discussing that salient issue. As history shows, office seekers often engage in powerful debate during these times. One telling example is the arguments over economic policy that occurred during the 1932 presidential race amid the Great Depression.

Similar conditions may not be equally momentous but may still produce more valuable discourse. If a particular theme captures the consciousness of the electorate, to the exclusion of other themes, candidates can only respond by discussing that theme. The crisis over health insurance that led to the defeat of Richard Thornburgh in the 1990 Pennsylvania Senate race serves as a good illustration of this phenomenon. For whatever reason, voters in that state were convinced that there was a major problem with the provision of medical assistance. In this situation, the health care issue moved to the forefront of voters' minds, dominating vote choice in such a way that the decisions of the persuadable voters turned on who could provide the best solution to the problem. Both candidates were effectively forced to discuss the issue, creating dialogue. As one would expect, the Democratic challenger, Harris Wofford, took a position that was closer to that of the median voter and thus, despite Thornburgh's responses, Wofford won. The point is that this one dimension so dominated public opinion that other communicative avenues were foreclosed.

While critical elections are rare, it may not be so unusual for one dimension to dominate campaign discussion. Table 7.5 details an attempt to isolate dominating issues across each of the forty-nine states in the sample. This table lists all the races and their total lines of discussion, then it highlights the most discussed dimension and the percentage of all discussion related to that dimension. The table is sorted by that percentage, from most to least dominating dimensions. The variation is substantial. At the top the issue of PACs dominated the 1988 race in Minnesota. Likewise, the dimensions of environment, crime, defense, the economy, and Welfare dominated the 1990 Oregon, the

Table 7.5 *Predominance of Leading Dimension's Discussion by Race (sorted)*

Race	Total Lines	Most Raised	Lines	Percent	Dialogue %	
					Inst.	Sust.
MI88	269	PACS	154	.57	5	23
OR90	4,597	ENV	2,233	.48	10	9
WA88	2,036	CRIME	879	.43	33	19
VA90	624	DEFEND	222	.35	35	23
PA92	4,593	ECON	1,563	.34	42	16
NY88	935	WELF	313	.33	20	14
KY92	210	PERF	67	.31	12	7
MN88	2,545	HEALTH	785	.3	21	13
MO88	724	SOCSEC	224	.3	13	4
MO92	797	HEALTH	243	.3	6	5
FL88	1,804	LIB	535	.29	0	4
GA92	994	PERF	298	.29	5	9
NJ88	1,157	ENV	345	.29	0	16
OH92	1,377	ABORT	389	.28	23	17
FL92	591	ECON	165	.27	28	5
KS90	506	TAX	137	.27	2	17
MA88	1,004	ECON	281	.27	28	18
TX90	1,038	SPEND	271	.26	12	8
IN92	1,754	TRADE	445	.25	35	16
NJ90	923	TAX	237	.25	37	16
IA92	794	PERF	195	.24	0	17
WA92	694	ECON	171	.24	16	12
NV92	952	PACS	227	.23	11	5
KY90	2,881	TAX	647	.22	22	3
OR92	3,043	ENV	675	.22	0	6
WI92	4,058	TAX	927	.22	16	12
IN90	1,193	ABORT	255	.21	22	17
MI90	1,176	TAX	248	.21	13	21
NC92	1,892	PERF	399	.21	18	15
CA88	2,479	ENV	499	.2	19	18
TX88	1,495	PERF	310	.2	9	15
AZ88	1,205	PERF	229	.19	0	17
IL90	1,121	EDUC	216	.19	48	4
KS92	607	PACS	121	.19	21	4
MA90	3,020	LIB	591	.19	9	10
MD92	1,267	PERF	253	.19	24	6
OH88	912	PERF	175	.19	33	26

Table 7.5   (*cont.*)

Race	Total Lines	Most Raised	Lines	Percent	Dialogue % Inst.	Sust.
OK92	2,073	ECON	407	.19	19	20
CO92	2,912	ABORT	549	.18	30	7
IL92	2,569	CRIME	469	.18	17	6
OK90	1,507	TAX	273	.18	14	8
NE90	3,334	PERF	576	.17	10	20
CT92	1,808	ECON	301	.16	25	22
NE88	4,436	CRIME	742	.16	50	10
NY92	2,124	LIB	358	.16	24	4
CO90	1,435	ENV	210	.14	26	10
MN90	2,391	PACS	327	.13	7	10
AZ92	2,369	PACS	291	.12	18	4
NC90	5,202	INTEG	561	.1	0	16
Minimum	210		67	.1	0	3
Maximum	5,202		2,233	.57	50	26
Average	1,825		428.32	.24	18	12

1988 Washington, the 1990 Virginia, the 1992 Pennsylvania and the 1988 New York races, respectively. In each of these six cases more than a third of all discussion was devoted to that one dimension. In contrast, for the bottom seven races, less than 17 percent of all discussion focused on the most often raised dimension.

Given the above discussion, we would expect the top six dimensions – the "critical" issues – to feature much more dialogue than their relatively less often discussed companions. As Figure 7.2 emphasizes, this is indeed the case. The level of dialogue increases dramatically as the issue becomes more critical. The typical opportunity features only 7 percent instant dialogue. On the other hand, the average level of instant dialogue increases for the forty-three most often raised but non-critical issues to almost 20 percent. Even more striking, on the critical issues the average level of dialogue is as high as 37 percent or over five times higher than the base rate. This result is highly statistically significant, $p < .01$. A similar increase is observed for sustained dialogue. From a low base rate of 4.4, the average level of sustained dialogue climbs to 18.2 and 15.6 for most raised and critical issues respectively. This result is also highly statistically significant, $p < .01$. Thus, we can

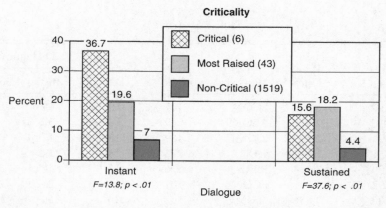

Figure 7.2 Critical dimensions and levels of dialogue (N = 1,568 instances).

provisionally conclude that issue criticality is a significant predictor of where dialogue will occur.

RACE INTENSITY

The model also makes assumptions about the agents in question. My model, for instance, examines the discourse created by equally advantaged candidates. This symmetry assumption made the model more parsimonious; however, it might also lead us to overlook some circumstances leading to campaign dialogue. In many American elections, candidates do not possess equivalent resources – one candidate is usually a frontrunner, more clearly advantaged from the outset. Somewhat paradoxically, this inequality is likely to lead to dialogue.

To rehearse this logic, the candidates' pursuit of electoral victory is the force that drives their behavior. Their focus on victory leads them to engage in the strategic message construction, which produces as its leading byproduct the avoidance of dialogue. In actual elections, some candidates cannot expect to win. In races involving these candidates, dialogue is more likely because whatever motivates these irrational – after all, why run if you have no chance of winning – candidates to run may impel them to speak on subjects which do not contribute to their vote total. Probably the best example of this is third-party candidates, but any candidate facing an entrenched incumbent would also illustrate this point. In this vein, scholars have observed the ability of third-party candidates to set the electoral agenda. The 1992 Perot campaign is a good example of this phenomenon. Perot was able to discuss the budget deficit to the point that it was taken up by the other campaigns.

Third-party candidates are not covered in my model, but we can imagine an analogous process occurring with poorly financed and therefore doomed challengers. There are many reasons why someone may run for office – to raise his or her stature for future elections, for example. In these cases, the candidate may do well to staunchly defend a minority-held position on a particular theme. For instance, late in the 1994 California race, after it was clear that she was going to lose, Kathleen Brown came out against Proposition 187, an anti-immigrant measure. She did this in order to shore-up support among Latinos in her constituency. In these instances, the irrational candidate plays into the stronger candidate's hands because it is easy for the stronger candidate to defend the majority position and thereby increase his or her vote total. Nevertheless, this condition can create dialogue in campaign discourse.

On the other hand, an alternative logic is also possible. The forces that produce good campaign discourse may encourage candidates in tighter races to dialogue more. Keeping in mind that campaign dialogue is a relatively rare occurrence, we are interested in the probability that at a given instance some dialogue will appear. The weaker candidate with respect to that dimension generally exercises this option. However, in races where candidates are more closely matched it is less likely that either candidate may be weaker and thus there may be a higher likelihood of dialogue. By another logic, the fact that both candidates are putting up a hard fight in the campaign may actually promote dialogue. Remember that the model specified decreasing marginal returns to resources spent on increasing salience. This means that at some point the candidates will have maximized the effective level of salience on particular dimensions. In this case, the minimal benefits from direct persuasion may be enough to push candidates to dialogue in these instances. In close contests this event is much more likely so we may expect to see more dialogue in close races.

To assess these contentions, I collected background data on each race. I employ three indicators to assess each candidate's chances of victory, which are presented in the upper panel of Table 7.6. First, victory margin provides a perfect, if ex post, measure of the candidates' electoral chances. This measure runs from .1, a race with the best possible chance for each candidate to .66 – a race where one candidate was completely blown out. This measure has a mean of .17 and a standard deviation of .14. Second, I coded for open seat races. It is a well-known

Table 7.6 *Descriptions of Indicators Used to Predict Dialogue's Appearance*

	Minimum	Maximum	Mean	Std. Deviation
Certainty of Victory				
Margin percent	.1	.66	.17	.14
Challenge	0	1	.86	.35
CQ intensity	1	4	2.2	.97
Candidate Positions				
Positional difference	0	9	4.3	1.97
Extreme	0	1	.34	.47
Dimension Type				
Hundreds of lines	0	22.32	.5704	1.2359
Owned	0	1	.3437	.4751
Dimension				
Consensual dimension	0	1	.3125	.4637
Critical dimension	0	1	.003	.001

fact that open seat races are much more likely to be intense than races with an incumbent and a challenger (Westlye 1991). A dummy variable taps whether there was an open seat; it is coded one if there is a challenger to an incumbent and zero otherwise. This measure has a mean of .86 and a standard deviation of .35. Finally, a third measure charts the predicted intensity of a race in the eyes of political experts. The magazine *Congressional Quarterly* regularly handicaps all senate races and, in that effort they have developed an indicator that runs from one, least intense, to four, most intense that is published long before election day in their round-ups. This measure has a mean of 2.2 and standard deviation of .97.

In all three cases the results of separate bivariate OLS regressions showed that level of dialogue increases as the intensity of race goes up. For margin, the level of dialogue decreases dramatically as the race becomes closer. The coefficients for instant dialogue and sustained dialogue are $-.11$ and $-.078$, respectively. This means that for every percentage increase in margin the average level of dialogue decreases by about a tenth of a percent. Both of these coefficients are statistically significant at p is less than .01 level. A similar pattern emerges for the challenger dummy variable. Here the coefficient for instant dialogue is $-.3$, which is significant at p is less than .05 level. For sustained dialogue the effect of challenger is not significant. Finally, for the *CQ* intensity measure, the effect is significant only for the amount of sustained dialogue. Here the coefficient is one, meaning that for each increase on their intensity scale, the amount of sustained dialogue goes up an average of one percent. This coefficient is significant at the .01 level. Thus, in four of six cases, the closeness of the race actually increases the chances for dialogue, while in the remaining two cases there is no discernible effect.

CANDIDATE POSITIONS

Dialogue may also occur as a function of the candidates' positions on a dimension. The model assumes that on every dimension one candidate is advantaged and the other is disadvantaged. However, the actual cases are more complex. The model has little to say about the size of the advantage. In keeping with the logic of irrational candidates discussed in the previous section, it may be that the farther apart the candidates the more likely dialogue is to occur. Thus, on some dimensions the advantage of the advantaged candidate is greater, less, or sometimes not present, and this may relate to the level of dialogue observed on that dimension. We can use the candidate positions data introduced above to see how these shifts in the candidates' positions relate to the presence of dialogue.

In a similar fashion, just as the candidates' relative positions influence dialogue so may the candidates's absolute positions. Specifically, we might expect more extreme candidates to be more likely to engage in dialogue, all else held equal. The rationale for this claim flows from the argument about irrational candidates. With a position far enough from the median voter, it becomes clear that the candidate is not interested in winning the race with respect to that position. In these cases the candidate is probably motivated by some other line of reasoning. The candidate may also do well to staunchly defend a minority-held position on a particular theme. Again, as with Kathleen Brown, the irrational candidate plays into the stronger candidate's hands because it is easy for the stronger candidate to defend the majority position and thereby increase his or her vote total. Nevertheless, this condition can create dialogue in campaign discourse.

I rearranged the data on candidate positions into two new variables to assess these possibilities. The first variable accounts for the differences in the candidates' positions. It is simply the absolute value of the mathematical difference between the two candidates' ratings on a given dimension. As the middle panel of Table 7.6 shows, this indicator runs from zero – the candidates have the same position – to nine, where the positions differ by the maximum amount. This measure has a mean of 4.3 and a standard deviation of 1.97. Another variable codes for extremity. This dichotomous measure (dummy variable) is coded one if a candidate within one and a half points either end of the position scale is present and zero otherwise.

In bivariate OLS regressions both of these measures influence the level of dialogue. For instant dialogue, the effect of positional differences is statistically significant but small. For every point increase in difference, the level of instant dialogue goes up by .008. Here the p level is .01. For sustained dialogue the effect is even greater. For every point increase in difference, the level of sustained dialogue goes up by .015. This effect is also significant at the .01 level. Thus, the wider the gap between candidates, the more likely dialogue is to appear.

The effect of extremity on instant dialogue is not statistically significant. On the other hand, the effect of extremity on sustained dialogue is significant at the .01 level. On average, extreme candidates are likely to produce .003 percent more dialogue than the rest. In the case of the relative gap, as well as in case of the absolute position of the candidates, those who are farther apart and at the extreme tend to produce more dialogue, on average. Further, the effect of the relative position is greater than that of the absolute position.

MULTIVARIATE PREDICTIONS OF DIALOGUE'S OCCURRENCE

Given these bivariate results, it is advisable to produce multivariate models in order to compare the degree of influence of all these factors on the rare appearances of dialogue in the Senate campaign content data. In this concluding section, all of the hypotheses tested thus far are combined into a single set of tests in order to make some definitive empirical claims. A full model is specified and estimated for levels of instant and sustained dialogue. After discussing these models, a full and reduced model is specified and estimated for the composite measure of dialogue constructed at the end of chapter six. This final model will produce an understanding of the dynamics of dialogue sufficient to ensure a reasonable degree of predictive validity as to when to expect dialogue in the future. The final model will also serve to summarize the results obtained in this chapter.

Table 7.7   *Predictors of Dialogue I*

		Percentage of Instant Dialogue	Percentage of Sustained Dialogue
	Hundreds of lines	5.82***	5.42***
Dimension	Owned dimension	−3.12***	−1.73***
Type	Consensual dimension	−3.56***	−.91*
	Critical dimension	56.22***	4.99
	Critical X lines	−7.52***	−4.98***
Certainty of	Margin percent	−9.87**	−3.74*
Victory	Challenge	−5.16***	−.11
	CQ intensity	−1.19*	.39
Candidate	Positional difference	.73**	.01
Positions	Extreme	−2.7**	.48
Region	Pacific	−1.58	−2.52**
	Mountain	−1.92	−.98
	West North Central	−.72	−.12
	East North Central	−.38	−1.3
	South	−5.53**	−1.3
	Mid-Atlantic	−3.33	−.6
	New England	2.51	.5
	Constant	14.32	2.86
	Adj. R-sq.	.11	.26
	N	1,568	1,568

Note: Asterisks indicate levels of statistical significance: ***$p < .01$; **$p < .05$; *$p < .1$.

Table 7.7 presents the results of two OLS regressions, estimating the influence of the indicators discussed above on the appearance of dialogue. The left-hand column investigates instant dialogue, and I will discuss it first. The indicators in this specification are taken from the discussion of the causes of dialogue above and simply rehearse the measures used thus far in the chapter. Once again, for the sake of convenience, Table 7.6 reports summary statistics for these measures. Three types of measures are detailed; one in each panel. The top panel reports on the data for certainty of victory, the middle for candidate positions, and the bottom for the type of dimension.

The multivariate regression (the left-hand column of Table 7.7) employs all of these indicators as well as a set of dummy variables representing region, which again acts as a proxy for editorial policy. This produces a specification of sixteen independent variables. I add an interactive term to this, which multiplies critical election and the number of lines. This term is discussed further below. Thus, the statistical model assesses the influence of each of these factors on the percentage of instant dialogue appearing while statistically controlling for all of the other factors.

The results are in line with what we would expect given the above discussion as the simultaneous controls do not change the estimates of the effects very much. The most basic predictor of the level of dialogue is the amount of overall discussion in a campaign. For every hundred lines of coverage the percentage of dialogue observed on average increases by almost 6 percent – an effect that is highly statistically significant (p < .01). Dimension type also represents a powerful and consistent set of influences. The three distinctions made above as to issue ownership, consensuality, and criticality all exert highly significant effects (p < .01). Being an owned issue or a consensual dimension works against observing dialogue. In each case the coefficient is close to 3 percent, meaning that for these dimension types the average amount of dialogue observed falls by almost half relative to the overall mean of roughly 7 percent.

Criticality exerts the greatest effect on increasing the level of dialogue. As the estimate in the left-hand column of Table 7.7 reveals, the average effect of being a critical dimension (controlling for all other factors) on the level of instant dialogue is over 56 percent. This factor, criticality, is sufficient to make for much more meaningful campaign discourse by itself, and without doubt it is the single largest effect in this specification. To put the magnitude of this estimate in perspective and compare it to the other most significant effect, an interactive term that multiplied criticality by the number of total lines in coverage of a race is also entered in this regression equation. (It should be noted that of all the interactive terms assessed, this was the only one with a consistent statistically significant impact.) The coefficient on the interaction is −7.52 meaning that in the presence of a critical election the increases in the number of lines cause the level of dialogue to fall by over 7 percent.

Figure 7.3 portrays the joint relationship, graphically. The predicted values of the interaction actually show that the amount of dialogue decreases as the number of lines increases; however, this finding is somewhat misleading. If we examine values that are closer to typical we see the importance of criticality in determining instant dialogue. The

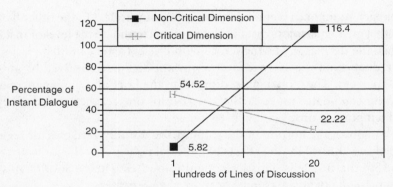

Figure 7.3 Predicted effect of coverage-criticality interaction on dialogue.

average amount of newspaper coverage across all instances is only fifty-four lines, on the other hand, the average amount of discussion for critical instances is 834 lines. Taking the predicted values, we see a few critical races with relatively little coverage and a lot of dialogue (52 percent on average) and the rest of the critical races with a higher but not extreme amount of coverage and only slightly less dialogue – about 22 percent on average.

The next group of indicators in the left-hand column of Table 7.7 estimates the effects of certainty of victory on the level of instant dialogue. All of these coefficients are statistically significant though not at the same high level as dimension type. Further, the effects are entirely negative, meaning they depress the amount of instant dialogue observed. For each percentage point increase in the electoral margin of the winning candidate, the amount of dialogue decreases an average of almost a tenth of one percent. Likewise, the presence of an incumbent–challenger race as opposed to an open seat decreases the level of instant dialogue by slightly over five percent. On the other hand, the more intense the race, the less instant dialogue appears. On average, a one-point climb in the four-point *CQ* intensity scale reduces the level of dialogue by one percent. However, this effect is swamped by the number of lines, which can also be seen as a measure of intensity, so, in general, the more certain the outcome of any given race, the less dialogue we see.

Moving to the candidate position data, again we see two statistically significant effects at the p < .05 level. On the one hand, the level of instant dialogue increases as the two candidates' positions move away from each other on that dimension. The increase is almost a percentage point for each point of movement on the nine-point scale. On the other hand, with a greater absolute distance by any one candidate the level of instant dialogue decreases. Having a race with one extreme candidate leads to a reduction in the average level of instant dialogue observed by about 2.7 percent. Thus, on a given dimension the level of dialogue increases as the candidates move farther apart until one reaches an extreme at which point it drops.

Finally, at the bottom of the column, the dummy variables for region used as a control for the effects of editorial policy, only the indicator for the Southern state is statistically significant. Being in the South tends to decrease dialogue an average of more than 5 percent.

Turning to the right-hand column of Table 7.7, we can inspect the same specification as it is used to estimate the effects of all the factors on the amount of sustained dialogue observed. The estimates closely parallel the ones achieved for instant dialogue, however, some are of smaller magnitude and not statistically significant. Moving from top to bottom, we can see that, due to the rarer appearance of sustained dialogue overall, having an owned or a consensual dimension exerts slightly less strong effects than they do for instant dialogue. Being an owned dimension decreases sustained dialogue an average of almost 2 percent while the effect of consensuality is not statistically significant. The effect of criticality and the number of lines is diminished, although the same pattern manifested in Figure 7.3 and the accompanying discussion once again appears.

Moving down, the effects of certainty of victory are all reduced with only the influence of margin being beyond chance. For every point increase in margin the level of sustained dialogue averages a .03 percent drop. The effects of the candidate positions are not significant, as well. For region, the only locale that experiences a statistically significant effect is the Pacific, where the amount of dialogue observed falls an average of two and a half points.

SUMMARY: THE COMPOSITE MEASURE

To summarize all these results, Table 7.8 presents estimates generated by the same specification on the composite measure of dialogue developed in chapter six. The regressions are presented in full and reduced form in the left- and right-hand column, respectively. The two equations' estimates are basically identical, so I will only go over the reduced form equation (the right-hand column) in detail.

Table 7.8   *Predictors of Dialogue II*

		Percentage of Composite Dialogue	Percentage of Composite Dialogue (Reduced)
	Hundreds of lines	7.11***	7.12***
Dimension	Owned dimension	−3.1***	−3.07***
Type	Consensual dimension	−2.3***	−2.1***
	Critical dimension	30.1***	29.57***
	Critical X lines	−7.53***	−7.51***
Certainty of	Margin percent	−7.64**	−5.54**
Victory	Challenge	−2.33**	−2.1**
	CQ intensity	−.15	
Candidate	Postional difference	.34*	.31*
Positions	Extreme	−.5	
Region	Pacific	−2.93*	−1.98*
	Mountain	−1.37	
	West North Central	−.12	
	East North Central	−1.05	
	South	−3.23**	−2.29**
	Mid-Atlantic	−1.81	
	New England	1.48	2.23*
	Constant	8.89	2.86
	Adj. R-sq.	.28	.28
	N	1,568	1,568

Note: Asterisks indicate levels of statistical significance: ***$p < .01$; **$p < .05$; *$p < .1$.

So, exactly what factors predict the rare occurrences of dialogue observed in the senate campaign data? There are basically four, editorial policy, dimension type, the certainty of victory, and the candidates' positions. The effect of editorial policy, as charted by its proxy of region, is important at the margins. Two regions – the Pacific and the South – display a statistically significant decrease, about two percentage points, in the amount of dialogue typically observed. At the same time, New England shows a slightly significant, $p < .1$, increase in the level of dialogue by the same two percentage points. In addition the sheer amount of coverage, measured in lines, is highly predictive of an increase in the level of dialogue. For every hundred lines of coverage, the amount of dialogue observed on average increases roughly seven percent.

Likewise, the type of dimension exerts an effect on dialogue's likelihood to appear. Both owned and consensual dimensions tend to feature about 3 percent less dialogue than their unowned and valenced counterparts. The most important effect in terms of size is the dimension's criticality. Critical dimensions are likely to feature a higher and much more sustained level of dialogue.

In contrast, increases in the certainty of one candidate's victory significantly decrease the average amount of dialogue observed. For both the margin of victory and the presence of an incumbent–challenger race, the level of dialogue goes down. Across the range of margins observed, the level of dialogue falls by at least .05 percent for each percentage point increase in the gap. Type of race compounds this effect. When an incumbent and challenger are present (as opposed to an open seat) a further reduction of 2 percent is typically observed in the amount of dialogue that appears. Finally as the candidates move farther apart along a dimension the amount of dialogue increases. For each point (on a ten-point scale) separating the two candidates, the amount of dialogue rises by almost a third of a percent on average.

Overall, given these four types of factors we can explain 28 percent in the variation of dialogue observed in these Senate races. This analysis provides some clues, which will be discussed further in the concluding chapter, as to the forces that can bring about more dialogue and better discourse in contemporary electoral campaigns.

CHAPTER 8

Conclusion: Toward More Substantive
Campaign Discourse

In this chapter, I summarize the findings of this project, focusing on my model of candidate behavior, the experimental results, and the correlational study of U.S. Senate campaigns. The model advances the understanding of elections, because it synthesizes formal work investigating candidate behavior with known empirical data on campaign communication effects and on voting behavior. The basic prediction is that there will be no obvious dialogue in mass elections. An extensive case study of the 1994 California gubernatorial election assessed this result. This race was well suited to the scientific study of dialogue because one candidate, Kathleen Brown, engaged her opponent in a dialogue on the subject of crime. The details concerning the failure of her campaign to secure electoral victory via this strategy corroborate the model.

The Senate campaign study examined the question of dialogue in more natural settings. It documented the rarity of dialogue in actual campaigns; then, after a closer examination of the model, it developed some hypotheses concerning when these rare instances of dialogue are likely to occur. The model highlights three categories of circumstances where dialogue is likely to occur. First, a particular newspaper's editorial policy may lead certain venues to provide better campaign coverage. Second, discussion of some types of dimensions, notably owned and consensual dimensions, are less likely to promote dialogue than others. Also in this category are the important environmental factors that produce critical elections, which are the most likely to feature dialogue and high-quality discourse. Third, there are violations of the models assumptions. Irrational candidates, those with less hope of winning, like challengers, or more extreme positions, are not as subject to the model's logical imperatives. For example, the level of dialogue increases dramatically, as the certainty of any one candidate will win the election goes down. In a related vein, candidates whose positions are closer together are more likely to dialogue.

Finally, I will raise another avenue that leads to better campaign discourse. The candidates may create a pseudodialogue, which I call reframing. The option of reframing lies somewhere in between responding and ignoring, so it is not as amenable to experimental or other study; however, it exists and represents a possibility for increasing the quality of discourse. Taken together with the idea that dialogue is rare, these situations constitute the primary conclusions of my project.

In this chapter, I will also discuss the application of my findings. In particular, I will address campaign reform. One of the most important implications of my research is that campaign reform, at least in its present guise, will do little or nothing to enhance the quality of political campaigns. In fact, my model suggests that equalizing access to financial resources will paradoxically decrease the level of dialogue across American political campaigns. I then challenge some of the assumptions about deliberative democracy raised in earlier chapters. Deliberative Democrats have excluded traditional advocacy groups, especially political parties, from their governmental ideal. It may well be that our polity would be better served by enhancing organizations designed to represent interests and reach political decisions in existing forums rather than attempting to create new deliberative enterprises at every level of society. Finally, I will talk about developments in communication technology, namely the Internet, which will likely lead to fundamental changes in the practice of political campaigns and challenge the foundations of the work I have presented.

PROJECT SUMMARY

The problem with which this project began was the lack of substance in contemporary political campaigns. One of the fundamental themes in the "American" approach to collective self-governance is the use of institutional incentives to turn private political ambition to public advantage. However, this route seems to have failed where political campaigning is concerned. Observers of elections have regularly complained that candidates ignore each other's rhetoric and talk past each other (Bryce 1895, cited in Kelley 1960; Berelson, Lazarsfeld, and McPhee 1954; Petrocik 1996).

I asserted that this lack of dialogue is largely responsible for campaigns that seem irrelevant and devoid of substance; further, I argued that the lack of campaign substance is increasingly detrimental to society. Recall that, "the quality of the making and of the defending of claims in the public sphere can be seen as a measure of society's success" (Kingwell 1995, p. 83). On a more pragmatic note, the disaffection that haunts our political system can be tied to the low quality of political campaigns (Ansolabehere and Iyengar 1995; Bennett 1992). The sea change in the conduct of national politics has changed the traditional competition between parties into a clash of candidates, and has made campaigns the public's primary link to government (Kernell 1988; Wattenberg 1986; Polsby 1983). Thus, I maintain that the research I have presented on the factors that can elevate campaign discourse is vital.

I developed a yardstick to measure the quality of political campaigns, which I called dialogue. My rationale for setting this standard relied heavily on classic and modern democratic theory. Mill's notion of a "marketplace of ideas," Habermas's "ideal speech situation," and others presume a requirement for effective public speech that basically calls for speakers to respect the audience by responding to what each other says. Dialogue occurs whenever speakers discuss the same subject. Put another way, when faced with another speaker's thematic initiative, a speaker can choose to ignore it and raise a different topic or can choose to respond on that subject. Ignoring the other speaker closes the door to meaningful communication while a response creates dialogue and fosters the debate that idealists envision. As a necessary condition for rational communication, the level of dialogue is a good indicator of the quality of the discourse, where more is better.

A MODEL OF CONTEMPORARY CAMPAIGNS

The concept of dialogue served as the departure point for my investigation of candidate behavior. I equated the decision to dialogue to a strategic choice, made in light of the candidates' expectations as to what responding to or ignoring a particular theme will do to their electoral prospects. Using the mathematical machinery of game theory, I developed a model that identifies the forces that act on candidates' choices over what themes to discuss in their campaign message. The model explains why dialogue seldom occurs. The model also highlights some rare circumstances that may bring about dialogue.

The model synthesized the literature on voting behavior, political communication, and candidate strategy. I asserted that there are an infinite number of potential considerations that may affect an individual's vote. These considerations correspond to topics the candidates can choose to discuss in the campaign. When candidates discuss a topic, they raise the importance or salience of that topic in the voters' minds, so voters weigh that consideration more heavily in deciding their vote. This critical premise concerning campaign communication is known as the priming effect (Iyengar and Kinder 1987; Krosnick and Kinder 1990). Rational candidates want to prime the topics they believe will enhance their electoral prospects.

The model resolved two questions. First, what themes should candidates discuss? The candidates' allocation strategies depend on the relative positions of the candidates. Following Black's (1958) logic, a candidate does best in terms of increasing expected vote by choosing to talk about those themes on which he or she is relatively closer to the median voter's expected position. Second, why do candidates avoid dialogue? Assuming their positions differ, only one candidate is advantaged on any theme and that candidate would like to discuss that theme because that message will increase the advantage. Because voters' weights can only increase as a result of campaign discussion, the advantage of the advantaged candidate will also increase if the other candidate responds by talking about that same theme. Thus, candidates will spend all their resources discussing themes where they are advantaged and none on themes where they are disadvantaged. So long as my assumptions hold, this result rules out the possibility for dialogue among strictly rational candidates.

There are two main differences between my formulation and other efforts to model campaigns. First, while candidates are understood to be strategic actors, voters are taken to behave sincerely. My alternative representation of vote choice conforms more closely to the well-researched portrayal of voting behavior (Campbell et al. 1960; Miller and Shanks 1996). Second, unlike existing models of the campaign, mine is multidimensional, which enables the study of salience effects.

EXPERIMENTAL RESULTS

The 1994 California gubernatorial election provided a unique opportunity to assess my model. The candidates in this race self-consciously believed in or rejected the vote-getting value of dialogue (Lubenow 1995). Given the Darwinian nature of politics, that is, the disappearance of unsuccessful techniques, this kind of clash is rare and, therefore, valuable for studying. A set of controlled experiments constituted the main portion of the case study. The experiments followed a naturalistic procedure. Adult participants viewed and responded to commercials actually employed by the candidates. Two experiments followed a two-ad design, charting the effects of twenty different pairings of candidate messages.

The model's central prediction is that the candidates' strategic calculus is responsible for diminishing the prospects for campaign dialogue. The two-ad experiments verified this result by demonstrating that voters penalize candidates who attempt to dialogue. On average, an ad devoted to dialogue cost the opting candidate one-fifth of the electorate compared to the best possible response. Similarly, an ad devoted to inoculation, a dialogue-enhancing strategy based on preempting an opponent's likely themes, typically cost the candidate a sixth of the electorate. The magnitude of these penalties may be exaggerated somewhat due to the experimental context, but their existence supports the inference that rational candidates would refrain from adopting dialogue-enhancing campaign strategies.

Senate Study

Picking up where the experiment left off, a correlational study of campaign discourse in U.S. Senate elections first confirmed that the overall level of dialogue in actual elections is low. The Senate study then took these rare instances of dialogue and, in combination with a closer examination of the model, developed some explanations for much of this dialogue. By doing so they identified some factors that could enhance the level of substance in contemporary campaigns. The model ignored the editorial processes underlying journalistic coverage of elections. And yet, as was demonstrated, there is some variance in the way different papers cover the elections. This observation leads to the conclusion that the media are at least partially responsible for the quality of campaign discourse. In addition, the model is predicated on the assumption that all dimensions are the same, the political environment is neutral, and those candidates are perfectly rational. However, in the real world of politics not all dimensions, times, and candidate pairings are created equal. Different types of dimensions seem more and less likely to foster dialogue. Special environmental circumstances can reduce the dimensions available for discussion and force dialogue on candidates. Moreover, the certainty of one candidate's victory can lead to the appearance of dialogue. All of these kinds of dialogue fall outside of the basic model's purview but is loosely explainable.

REFRAMING

The most interesting prospect for dialogue and for future research into campaign communication is the notion of reframing, discussion of which has been left until this point. Reframing involves a shift in dimensions in response to an opponent's thematic initiative. When a candidate lies about an opponent's record, for instance, this kind of response seems to be the most advantageous. Dialogue has the detrimental effects of propagating and increasing attention to the lie, but this effect may be outweighed, in the attacked candidate's view, by the damage done to the opponent's credibility. To consider another example, imagine an opponent attacks a candidate with a charge of tax evasion. The attacked candidate may likely respond by saying that he has always paid his rightful tax bill, but he may also counterattack the opponent for engaging in sleazy campaigning. In a classic rhetorical maneuver, the candidate has moved the debate away from the opponent and onto his ground.

The nature of the response is intriguing. The first part of the response is dialogue in that it answers directly to a claim. The second part of the response does not constitute dialogue as others and I typically define it. The shift to the character dimension brings a new topic to the discourse. A suitable empirical analysis would measure the relative weight of these themes in the response to chart the precise level of dialogue. Of course, this point presumes that these themes are analytically separable. The shift in politics is often more subtle and occurs at a less obvious level. The interesting issue involves the construction of thematic dimensions in the collective mind of the electorate.

In the 1992 debate over family values, for instance, the Democrats did a masterful job of shifting the dimension onto a new axis. When this theme emerged in Republican rhetoric, it was associated with pro-marriage proposals and quasireligious themes like prayer in schools. These underlying policy measures enjoyed majority support and consequently the rhetoric, which led to increasing the salience of this issue, increased the amount of support voters awarded to Republican candidates. The Democrats responded with a message that did not quite create a dialogue but certainly did not completely ignore the Republican message. They redefined family values to include subdimensions where their policies were more in line with the median, such as parental leave and better childcare. This exercise in reframing shifted the advantage conferred by family values' increased salience by reshuffling the electorate's preferences with respect to that theme.

Such an instance arose again in the presidential election of 2000. Even a casual observer would note that the two candidates, George W. Bush and Al Gore, seemed to address the same themes at some points. Most notably the candidates both discussed the themes of tax cuts and social security policy. Now it may well be that this was genuine dialogue prompted by the fact that the candidates' positions were equidistant from the median voter. There is also some indication that the candidates were engaged in reframing. For example, although Bush and Gore both raised the problem of social security, they raised different subdimensions in facing this topic. Bush reminded voters of his idea to privatize a portion of the benefits while Gore brought up the idea of a "lockbox." In this way the question of social security was at least partially better developed for the voters and the campaign took on some semblance of meaningful discussion. In general, these possibilities for a form of quasidialogue represent the brightest avenue for future study.

THE SHAPE OF DELIBERATIVE DEMOCRACY

This project has attempted to raise new concerns about the nature of political legitimacy in a complex democratic society. I will briefly contrast the ideal of deliberative democracy raised previously with the reality of mass political participation in the current sociopolitical milieu. In my view, the notion of deliberation as it has been articulated thus far provides only a partial answer to the question of how to govern a society as large and complex as ours. Unless fostered and channeled through political institutions, deliberation may be far too tenuous in practice or far too demanding a requirement to meet. On the other hand, the system of institutions one could imagine necessary to further the deliberative democrat's ideal seems to resemble the strong system of party governance already advocated by many political scientists. The concept of deliberation may be superfluous in that it merely reinforces our collective desire to reinvigorate existing institutions, like parties.

It is common for deliberative democrats to put forth a vision of an ideal world in which everyone participates in a political discourse that collectively results in legitimate public policy. However, those seeking realistic reform must ask where such deliberation would occur and who would do it. For example, Michael Walzer (1989–90) proposed the idea of "microspheres," a multitude of small arenas in which groups of people create political discourse that is incorporated, "bubbling up," into larger discursive groups until it reaches the entire polity. It is perhaps too easy to argue that to expect every American citizen to participate in such groups is beyond realistic. The cognitive and motivational limits on the participation of citizens in everyday governance are too well known. In the contemporary situation, even important (and well-structured) decisions, such as voting for the President, are rarely seriously considered by even a majority of the polity, and that estimate is probably generous.

Of course, deliberation and participation should be encouraged, as deliberative democrats say, through education and adequate forums. This call to increased political activity is hardly radical. A realistic notion of democracy must account for the fact that the task of deliberation is hard. It is so hard, in fact, that it is probably not reasonable to expect more than a small number of people to actually do it. Further, whether the act of deliberation is construed as a right or a duty, the polity is unable to compel individuals to deliberate on command. We are necessarily left with a civil discourse that is created only through the voluntary participation of a potentially apathetic public.

The advocates of deliberative democracy may respond that a principled hearing on the issue at hand is enough to satisfy the requirements of the ideal. This argument presumes that people are open to decisions and politics that run against their interests and beliefs so long as the decision process is fair. In some circumstances this may be true, but in others it may not. Groups advocating a minority-held view that is repeatedly rejected may well come to doubt the wisdom of their participation in the deliberative enterprise and withdraw. One question that must be posed and tested in the real world concerns the strength of the commitment to deliberation itself as compared to the commitment to particular beliefs and policies.

Thus, in a world where participation in deliberation is voluntary, citizens will disagree and outcomes are ultimately decided by majority rule, what are we left with? Given that the spirit of the one-person one-vote rule means that number matters, we would first observe the tendency for like-minded people to band together to advocate their positions more forcefully. Thus, these three points immediately give rise to the entire gamut of interest group politics. No deliberative democrat has precluded the possibility of bargaining and coalition formation from deliberation, so it is likely that in the face of specific political decisions these groups would coalesce to form umbrella groups seeking to win majority support.

How is this simple scheme any different from the notion of parties common to political science? The notion of deliberative democracy is not only compatible with the notion of active parties; it may well be identical. The upshot is that deliberative democrats are left with the same problem I have tried to address, how institutional incentives can lead privileged communicators to dialogue before large audiences.

IMPLICATIONS FOR CAMPAIGN REFORM

Given the almost contempt with which the American public holds contemporary campaign discourse, it is not surprising that there are many public policy efforts afoot to elevate the level of discussion in campaigns. In this section, I will apply my findings to this chronic and hotly debated political issue of campaign reform. Most reform measures focus on placing limits on spending in the hope of reducing the need for funds and equalizing communication resources available across candidates. These reforms may have positive effects, freeing officeholders from the onerous task of raising money and breaking the potentially corrupting link between campaign donations and public policy. However, my investigation clearly indicates that these reforms, by themselves, would do nothing to increase the substantive content of campaigns. My research is particularly germane where equalizing resources is concerned.

The McCain–Feingold bill currently on the floor of the U.S. Senate is a prototypical example of the campaign reform. Without going into detail, it would place stricter limits on the amount of money spent by each candidate in each race. It would also subsidize campaign communication by encouraging owners of media resources to donate airtime or charge lower rates to political candidates during the campaign season. Embedded in this proposal and others like it is the idea that communication resources would be equalized across candidates. Under this proposal incumbents would not be able to outspend challengers by ratios of three or four to one, a pattern that has been common in recent years (Jacobson 1983). The government, in the name of campaign regulation, would take steps to ensure a fair communicative fight, where fair means both candidates are able to devote the same amount of money to sending their campaign messages.

My model is also predicated on equal access to resources, and all the findings hold with this condition in mind. Thus, there is at least one strong correspondence between the research presented in this project and the actuality of political campaigns should McCain–Feingold style reform be enacted. My work has demonstrated that even in this potentially improved campaigning environment there is no reason to expect any improvement in the quality of campaign discourse. Kathleen Brown did not lose the election because of lack of money. She lost because of her strategic choice. Even with equal access to funds, there will be little dialogue. Somewhat paradoxically, as I argued in the previous section, campaign reform of this kind may actually decrease the level of dialogue. One of the situations I discussed involved poorly financed challengers raising minority-held views. Equalizing resources across candidates would tend to reduce this opportunity for the creation of dialogue.

Similarly, proposals to cap the amount of soft money would also diminish the prospects for dialogue. Soft money is a donation given to parties rather than candidates, which is unregulated by current law. Parties tend to allocate this money toward the discussion of themes that they believe will benefit their candidate in particular elections. Regulating soft money would lead to a more equitable distribution of funds across candidates in each election. By the logic outlined above, this would decrease the amount of dialogue. In addition, the regulation of soft money would further disrupt the parties' role in elections and, as discussed in the previous section on deliberative democracy, weakening political parties is not likely to have a beneficial impact on the quality of public discourse.

Instead of campaign finance, my investigation highlights the importance of the electorate's reactions and the political environment. It would seem that the leading cause of the lack of dialogue is the fact that salience overwhelms content. To argue against a majority-held political point is typically electoral suicide. More electoral responsiveness to content within a given dimension and less flexibility in salience between dimensions seems to represent the right ingredients for a solution to the problem of encouraging substantive campaigns. The forces shaping political enthronement are also important. When organizations like strong parties reduce the dimensionality of the rhetorical space, clearer discourse ensues. In the absence of strong parties, this role can be played haphazardly by events and long-term political tides, but other organizations like the media and interest groups could be watchdogs that are more self-conscious about this process.

THE EVOLVING WORLD OF POLITICAL COMMUNICATION

In conclusion, I consider the robustness of my findings, especially the application of campaign research in light of the evolution of communication technology. The new century is witnessing an ongoing revolu-tion in communication technology that rivals the introduction of the printing press in terms of its impact on society. Without going deeply into the kind of metatheorizing that characterizes critical theory on communication and technology, I will attempt to make a simple obser-vation. Specifically, the growth of the Internet will change mass com-munication. I will then pose a few questions concerning the viability of the model of campaigns I have offered in the next era of human communication.

The signal characteristic of the Internet is its ability to host many-to-many communication at will. In contrast to the telephone system, which allows only one-to-one communication, or the system of broad-casting, which allows one-to-many communication, the Internet allows virtually anyone to communicate with everyone. There are fundamen-tal technical and psychological challenges posed by this kind of com-municative access, but let's assume that these issues can be resolved. What would such a system of individual-initiated mass broadcast-ing and interaction do to existing political regimes? Advocates of direct democracy expect devolution of governmental decision-making authority. Referenda, electronic town meetings, and the like would, in their vision, allow the public to make decisions in the absence of rep-resentation. The center of political gravity may move from a core of elites largely based in Washington D.C. to a widely dispersed and decen-tralized system of chat rooms and newsgroups only loosely connected and weakly organized. It is unlikely, however, that every citizen will par-ticipate in every decision. A preliminary question political science needs to address is what level of participation could the polity support?

The more relevant questions concern the shape of electoral cam-paigns. It seems likely that under any communication regime, day-to-day decisions would have to be made by elected officeholders acting as executives or meeting in representative bodies. It follows, then, that there would be candidates for these offices and preelection campaigns. The most drastic change would be that the privileged access that comes from major party nomination would diminish. It may not disappear, however, because securing something akin to a nomination may be nec-essary to generate the necessary legitimacy to gain attention. Neverthe-less, I would expect the relationship between candidates and voters to change. Little mediation, for example, would be needed, and voters would presumably be able to publicize their concerns in such a way that the candidates would be forced to answer. The agenda-setting power of the candidate would disappear, and with that change, the model I have presented would move toward obsolescence.

Perhaps the most important intellectual thread connecting the various approaches to studying mass political behavior is what Dewey called "the problem of the public." How can a mass of people govern themselves? The answer, of course, involves the separation into the government and the governed, which is carefully attenuated by mechanisms that ensure the legitimacy of governmental actions. My study has shown how to think about one of these institutions – the political campaign – within the critical arena of public discourse. I have developed a model that, for now, is fairly realistic. The model explains the lack of dialogue in relatively concrete terms. My theoretical analysis is supported by a case study involving novel as well as traditional methodologies. More work needs to be done. The few areas I have discussed in this conclusion seem to supply ample nourishment for the study of campaign effects, institutions of political discourse, and the linkages between formal and informal aspects of our political system.

Appendix A
Analysis of the Model of Campaigns
in Mass Elections

STRUCTURE OF THE GAME

P is an array of two dimensions. It represents public opinion – the themes that constitute the political environment in which the electorate and the candidates operate. The two dimensions are bounded by negative one and one, and they are indexed by $j = 1, 2$. The model can be generalized to more than two dimensions, but in the interest of simplicity only the case with two dimensions is considered. There is one voter who has an ideal point P_j on each dimension. These ideal points are distributed uniformly on the interval negative one and one, so they have an expected value of zero. Voter ideal points are independent across dimensions. The model can also be generalized to multiple voters.

There are two candidates indexed by k, $k = D, R$. Each candidate has an ideal point on each dimension P_{jk}. These ideal points are constrained to the "left" and "right": $P_{jD} \in [-1,0]$ and $P_{jR} \in [0,1]$. Each candidate has a budget B and makes allocations B_{jk} from that budget to the dimensions each chooses to discuss. These allocations are constrained: $B_{1k} + B_{2k} = B$ and $B_{jk} \geq 0$.

The voter chooses between the two candidates according to a voting strategy V. The candidate who receives the vote wins and sets policies equal to their ideal points $P_j{}^*$. Thus, if D wins $P_j{}^* = P_{jD}$ and if R wins $P_j{}^* = P_{jR}$.

THE VOTER'S UTILITY
The voter's overall utility from electing a particular candidate $U_{voter,k}$ depends on the utility derived from each dimension. The voter also weights each dimension according to a weight ω_{jk}:

(1) $U_{voter,k} = \omega_{1k}U_{1k} + \omega_{2k}U_{2k}$.

The voter's utility on each dimension U_{jk} is less as their position diverges from that of the candidates. The function is quadratic:

(2) $U_{jk} = -(P_j - P_{jk})^2$

For each dimension, the weight ω_j is proportional to total spending on dimension j $\dfrac{B_{jD} + B_{jR}}{2B}$. The effect of spending is also modified by another parameter, α, which reflects the marginal return to the campaign from increasing spending, in other words the elasticity of advertising expenditures (Hirschleifer 1989). With $0 \leq \alpha \leq 1$, there are decreasing marginal returns to campaign spending:

(3) $\omega_j = \left(\dfrac{B_{jD} + B_{jR}}{2B} \right)^{\alpha}$, where $0 \leq \alpha \leq 1$.

THE CANDIDATES' UTILITY

Candidate k's utility U_k depends on the winner's implemented policy P_j^* in the same fashion as the voter (save that there are no weights):

(4) $U_k = -(P_1 - P_1^*)^2 + -(P_2 - P_2^*)^2$

Thus it is easy to see that the candidate's utility is at a maximum when they win and at a minimum when they lose. Because a candidate either wins or loses depending on if they receive the vote, the candidate's utility is linked to the voter's utility. The candidate associated with the higher level of voter utility wins.

PLAY OF THE GAME

Play proceeds in the following sequence:

1. Nature draws voter ideal points, initial weights, and candidate positions.
2. Candidates allocate their budgets toward dimensions.
3. The voter chooses either candidate D or candidate R.
4. One of the candidates wins.
5. The winner implements ideal points as policy.

INFORMATION

The voter knows his or her ideal points as well as the candidates' ideal points and the budget allocations.

The candidates know their ideal points and budget allocations but only know the distribution of the voter's ideal points.

EQUILIBRIUM DEFINITION AND CHARACTERIZATION

The voter's equilibrium voting strategy V^* depends on the candidates' budget allocations and the parameters of the game, specifically the voter's and candidates' ideal points.

Candidate k's equilibrium budget allocation strategy B^*_{jk} maximizes the likelihood of receiving the vote. B^*_{jk} is a best response to the voter and the other candidate, so candidate strategy is a function of the voter's candidates' ideal points. Thus, the equilibrium is a set consisting of a voting strategy and two candidate allocation strategies, $\{V^*, B^*_D, B^*_R\}$ where: V^* maximizes $U_{voter,k}$, B^*_D maximizes U_D, and, B^*_R maximizes U_R.

Equilibrium Strategies

The equilibrium strategy for the voter is to vote for the candidate associated with the greatest utility. From equation 1 and (noncritically) giving D the vote in the case of ties.

(5) V^* = choose D   if $\omega_{1D}U_{1D} + \omega_{2D}U_{2D} \geq \omega_{1R}U_{1R} + \omega_{2R}U_{2R}$
         choose R   otherwise.

Using backwards induction, we can derive the candidates' optimal choices from the voter's strategy. Here I will solve the game only for candidate D as R's choices are symmetrical. D's maximization problem is to maximize $\omega_{1D}U_{1D} + \omega_{2D}U_{2D} - \omega_{1R}U_{1R} + \omega_{2R}U_{2R}$. As D only has control over his or her own budget allocations D wants to maximize equation 6 with respect to B_1 and B_2:

(6) $\underset{B_1 \& B_2}{Max}(\omega_{1D}U_{1D} + \omega_{2D}U_{2D}) - (\omega_{1R}U_{1R} + \omega_{2R}U_{2R}).$

This maximization is performed using Lagrange's technique. Substituting equation 2 and equation 3 into equation 6 yields (factoring the weights)

(7) $\underset{B_1 \& B_2}{Max} E\left(\left(\frac{B_{1D} + B_{1R}}{2B}\right)^\alpha\right)\left((P_1 - P_{1R})^2 - (P_1 - P_{1D})^2\right)$

$+\left(\left(\frac{B_{2D} + B_{2R}}{2B}\right)^\alpha\right)\left((P_2 - P_{2R})^2\right) - \left((P_2 - P_{2D})^2\right)\right)$

where E is an expectation operator.

Adding the budget constraint to equation 7 produces the Lagrangian function. (The equation is also reduced given the voter's ideal points are independent and their expected value is zero.)

$$(8) \quad L = \left(\left(\frac{B_{1D} + B_{1R}}{2B}\right)^{\alpha}\right)\left(P_{1R}^{\,2} - P_{1D}^{\,2}\right) + \left(\left(\frac{B_{2D} + B_{2R}}{2B}\right)^{\alpha}\right)\left(P_{2R}^{\,2} + P_{2D}^{\,2}\right)$$
$$+ \lambda((B_{1D} + B_{2D}) - B)$$

There are three first-order conditions, one for each dimension and one for the budget constraint. The first two conditions are:

$$(9a) \quad \frac{\partial L}{\partial B_{1D}} = \frac{\alpha}{2B}\left(\frac{B_{1D} + B_{1R}}{2B}\right)^{\alpha-1}\left(P_{1R}^{\,2} - P_{1D}^{\,2}\right) + \lambda$$

$$(9b) \quad \frac{\partial L}{\partial B_{2D}} = \frac{\alpha}{2B}\left(\frac{B_{2D} + B_{2R}}{2B}\right)^{\alpha-1}\left(P_{2R}^{\,2} - P_{2D}^{\,2}\right) + \lambda$$

The final condition is the budget constraint

$$(10) \quad \frac{\partial L}{\partial \lambda} = B_{1D} + B_{2D} - B$$

Setting the two first order conditions equal to each other produces the following requirement for D's optimal allocations.

$$(11) \quad \left(\frac{B_{2D} + B_{2R}}{B_{1D} + B_{1R}}\right)^{\alpha-1} = \frac{P_{1R}^{\,2} - P_{1D}^{\,2}}{P_{2R}^{\,2} - P_{2D}^{\,2}}$$

Thus, spending along any dimension will be proportional to the difference in the candidates' positions. (It is easy to see that the voter's strategy is optimal by solving for the allocation vectors and plugging them into the voter's utility function.) By the same logic, the condition to maximize R's utility is symmetric.

How does this condition dictate candidate k's budget allocations? After accounting for α, as $P_{1R}^{\,2} - P_{1D}^{\,2}$ increases, either because R is further or D is closer to the expected position of the median voter, the budget allocation D wants to make to dimension 1 increases and the budget allocation D wants to make to dimension 2 decreases.

DIALOGUE

This result, together with the budget constraint, leads directly to the proposition that rational candidates will avoid dialogue. Dialogue is defined as

(12) if $B_{jD} > 0$ then $B_{jR} > 0$ and vice versa

Thus, if either D or R spend any money on a dimension, then the other candidate will also spend money on that dimension. Equation 11 demonstrates that with any difference between dimensions, candidates will shift their campaign spending away from the dimension on which they are disadvantaged and toward the dimension on which they are advantaged. In fact, each candidate would prefer to spend increasing amounts on one dimension and decreasing amounts on the other.

Given the budget constraints, however, the actual allocation is a corner solution. With two candidates the shifting occurs simultaneously, again assuming $P_{jR}^2 - P_{jD}^2$ is distinct across dimensions; each candidate would allocate all their resources to the more favorable dimension and none to the other dimension, which would be left to the opponent. Thus, the equilibrium prediction is that there will be no campaign dialogue.

Appendix B
Experimental Procedures

PARTICIPANTS

The experiments took place during the 1994 California gubernatorial race, from September 4 to November 2. Using several methods, including newspaper advertisements and flyers, 604 adults were recruited from the local community. They were promised a payment of $10 in return for engaging in an hour-long study of "selective perception." Although the sample was obviously nonrandom, participants reflected the composition of California. Across all the experiments, 58 percent of the participants were male, 51 percent were white, 21 percent were black, 10 percent were Asian, and 12 percent were Hispanic. The median age was 35. Thirty-eight percent of the participants claimed affiliation with the Democratic party, 31 percent were Republicans, and 18 percent claimed to be independents (the balance did not report an affiliation). Fifty-five percent were college graduates, with the rest being evenly divided between high school graduates and individuals with some college. To compensate for selection biases, the analyses were repeated after weighting the sample to match statewide proportions; however, this procedure did not materially alter any of the results.

PROCEDURE

The experiments were conducted at two separate locations, one in West Los Angeles and one in Los Angeles's downtown area. The former is a heavily Democratic area, the latter, a more cosmopolitan urban center. The experimental facilities in both locations consisted of a three-room office suite with two viewing rooms and a separate area for questionnaire completion. The experimental setting replicated a natural television viewing experience as faithfully as possible. The lab approximated a home-viewing environment with couches, easy chairs, and coffee tables. Most subjects came with friends or work associates, adding an air of informality to the viewing sessions. Standard televisions and videocassette recorders were used to reinforce this feeling.

When participants telephoned the facility, they were scheduled for a time of their choice. The typical session included two or three participants. On arrival, subjects were given a set of directions that disguised the true purpose of the study, telling them that it concerned selective perception of local newscasts. They then completed a short pretest questionnaire concerning their social background, media activities, and political interest. All dependent measures were contained in the post-test in order to avoid forewarning the subjects as to the study's political purpose. After completion of the pretest, participants were taken to a viewing room. Subjects saw a twelve-minute videotape of a recent local newscast (described to participants as having been selected at random), which was professionally edited to include two breaks with three thirty-second commercials in each. Depending upon the randomly assigned condition, from zero to two political spots were substituted for the regular ads. These spots were actual campaign advertisements, which were procured from the candidates or taped from local broadcasts. Transcripts of these ads are available from the author upon request.

Following the tape's completion, participants completed a lengthy post-test questionnaire which tapped their beliefs and opinions on a wide range of campaign issues, including the dependent measures used below. Additional items concerning local media figures and nonpolitical issues were added as padding in order to ensure that subjects did not discover the true purpose of the study. On completion of the post-test, participants were debriefed according to American Psychological Association guidelines and paid.

MEASURES

In the pretest, partisanship was tapped by, "Generally speaking, do you think of yourself as a Republican, a Democrat, an independent, or what?" In the analysis, responses were coded: one for Democrat; zero for independent, other, or missing data; and negative one for Republican.

In the post-test, three batteries measured subjects' beliefs about their own issue stances and those of the candidates. The self-placements were prefaced by, "Next, we would like to know where you stand on various political issues. For each of the following issues, indicate your position, using the scales shown below. For example, if you were pro-choice, you would circle one or two. If you don't know, please circle the number nine." The issues and endpoint label of the five-point scales were as follows (words substituted into the other endpoint appear in parentheses): Immigration, Favor strong (oppose any) action to limit the flow of illegal immigrants. Education, Favor (oppose) increased government spending on public schools. Three strikes – the crime question – Strongly favor (oppose) the Three-strikes idea. For the candidate placements, Kathleen Brown and Pete Wilson were substituted in the introductory statement, and their names were included in the scale labels. All the "don't know" responses were excluded from the analysis. Otherwise, the scales were recoded as indicated.

The priming analysis employed better job questions. These questions were presented in a battery prefaced by, "For each of the following state problems, please indicate which of the gubernatorial candidates is more likely to produce results." The education question read, "Improving the quality of our public schools." The crime question read, "Reducing the crime rate." The economy question read, "Promoting economic growth and employment." The immigration question read, "Preventing illegal immigration." The response set was the same for all questions: Kathleen Brown, Pete Wilson, and about the same/unsure. Except where noted Brown was coded one; about the same, zero; and Wilson negative one. The vote was measured by asking, "How will you vote in the gubernatorial election?" and coded one for Kathleen Brown, zero for undecided or other, and negative one for Wilson.

ESTIMATION

Two kinds of estimation procedures were used in the analysis. The statistical significance of differences in mean values was assessed using a two-tail T-test, and the T-statistic is reported in parentheses. Other analyses all take advantage of OLS multiple regression techniques. In these cases a logistic specification would be more appropriate technically, but would make the interpretation of coefficients more difficult, and in any case the substantive results are similar. The regression specifications all followed the same basic format: $B1^*$ condition $+ B2^*$

participant's partisanship = gubernatorial vote. Condition was coded as a dichotomy with zero representing the control group and one representing the relevant treatment condition. Partisanship and gubernatorial voter were scored as indicated above.

References

Aldrich, John. 1995. *Why Parties? The Origin and Transformation of Political Parties in America.* Chicago: University of Chicago Press.

Alexander, Herbert. 1992. *Financing Politics: Money, Elections and Political Reform.* Washington D.C.: CQ Press.

Anderson, Norman. 1966. Component ratings in impression formation. *Psychonomic Science* 6:179–80.

Ansolabehere, Steve and Shanto Iyengar. 1995. *Going Negative: How Attack Ads Shrink and Polarize the Electorate.* New York: The Free Press.

Ansolabehere, Steve, Roy Behr, and Shanto Iyengar. 1993. *The Media Game: American Politics in the Television Age.* New York: Macmillan.

Ansolabehere, Steve, Shanto Iyengar, Adam Simon, and Nicholas Valentino. 1994. Do negative campaigns demobilize the electorate? *American Political Science Review* 84:829–38.

Arrow, Kenneth. 1951. *Social Choice and Individual Values.* New York: Wiley.

Austen-Smith, David. 1990. Information transmission in debate. *American Journal of Political Science* 34:124–52.

Axelrod, Robert. 1970. *Conflict of Interest.* Chicago: Markham Press.

Banks, Jeffrey. 1990. A model of electoral competition with incomplete information. *Journal of Economic Theory* 50:309–25.

Barber, Benjamin. 1984. *Strong Democracy: Participatory Politics for a New Age.* Berkeley: University of California Press.

Bartels, Larry. 1993. Messages received: political impact of media exposure. *American Political Science Review* 2:267–85.

Becker, Gary. 1996. *Accounting for Tastes.* Cambridge: Harvard University Press.

Bennett, Lance. 1992. *The Governing Crisis: Media, Money, and Marketing in American Elections.* New York: St. Martin's Press.

    1996. *News: The Politics of Illusion.* New York: Longman Press.

Berelson, Bernard, Paul Lazarsfeld, and William McPhee. 1954. *Voting: A Study of Opinion Formation in a Presidential Campaign.* Chicago: University of Chicago Press.

Bernhardt, Marcus and Daniel Ingberman. 1985. Candidate reputations and the incumbency effect. *Journal of Public Economics* 27:47–67.

Bessette, Joseph. 1994. *The Mild Voice of Reason: Deliberative Democracy and American National Government.* Chicago: University of Chicago Press.

Black, Duncan. 1958. *The Theory of Committees and Elections.* Cambridge: Cambridge University Press.

Bohman, John. 1996. *Public Deliberation: Pluralism, Complexity and Democracy.* Cambridge: MIT Press.

Brody, Richard and Benjamin Page. 1972. The assessment of policy voting. *American Political Science Review* 66:450–58.

Buchanan, Bruce. 1991. *Electing a President.* Austin: University of Texas Press.

Budge, Ian and David Farlie. 1983. *Explaining and Predicting Elections: Issue Effects and Party Strategies in Twenty-Three Democracies.* New York: Allen and Unwin.

Burnham, Walter. 1970. *Critical Elections and the Mainsprings of American Politics.* New York: Norton.

Calvert, Randall. 1986. *Models of Imperfect Information in Politics.* New York: Harwood.

Campbell, Angus, Phillip Converse, Warren Miller, and Donald Stokes. 1960. *The American Voter.* New York: Wiley.

Campbell, Donald and John Stanley. 1967. *Experimental and Quasi-Experimental Designs.* New York: Rand McNally.

Chambers, Simone. 1996. *Reasonable Democracy: Jurgen Habermas and the Politics of Discourse.* Ithaca: Cornell University Press.

Cappella, Joseph and Kathleen Jamieson. 1997. *Spiral of Cynicism: The Press and the Public Good.* Oxford: Oxford University Press.

Cohen, Joshua. 1989. Deliberation and democratic legitimacy, in Allan Hamlin and Phillip Pettit eds. *The Good Polity: Normative Analysis of the State.* Oxford: Basil Blackwell.

Converse, Phillip. 1964. The nature of belief systems in mass publics, in David Apter ed. *Ideology and Discontent.* New York: Free Press.

Converse, Phillip and George Markus. 1979. Plus ca change . . . *American Political Science Review* 73:2–49.

Dahl, Robert. 1989. *Democracy and Its Critics.* New Haven: Yale University Press.

Downs, Anthony. 1957. *An Economic Theory of Democracy.* New York: Harper and Row.

Dryzek, John. 1990. *Discursive Democracy: Politics, Policy and Political Science.* Cambridge: Cambridge University Press.

Edelman, Murray. 1988. *Constructing the Political Spectacle.* Chicago: University of Chicago Press.

Ehrenhalt, Alan. 1991. *The United States of Ambition.* New York: Times Books.

Enelow, James and Melvin Hinich. 1982. Nonspatial candidate characteristics and electoral competition. *Journal of Politics* 44:115–30.

Epstein, Edward. 1973. *News from Nowhere: Television and the News.* New York: Random House.

Ferejohn, John and Jim Kuklinski. 1990. *Information and Democratic Processes.* Urbana: University of Illinois Press.

Finkel, Steve. 1993. Reexamining the minimal effects model in recent Presidential campaigns. *Journal of Politics* 1:21.

Fiorina, Morris. 1981. *Retrospective Voting in American National Elections.* New Haven: Yale University Press.

Fishkin, James. 1991. *Democracy and Deliberation: New Directions for Democratic Reform.* New Haven: Yale University Press.

1992. *The Dialogue of Justice.* New Haven: Yale University Press.

1997. *The Voice of the People.* New Haven: Yale University Press.

Fiske, Susan and Shelley Taylor. 1991. *Social Cognition.* New York: McGraw-Hill.

Fowler, Linda and Robert McClure. 1989. *Political Ambition: Who Decides to Run for Congress.* New Haven: Yale University Press.

Franklin, Charles. 1994. Eschewing obfuscation? campaigns and the perception of U.S. Senate incumbents. *American Political Science Review* 85:1193–214.

Galston, William. 1991. *Liberal Purposes: Goods, Virtue and Diversity in the Liberal State.* New York: Columbia University Press.

Gans, Herbert. 1979. *Deciding What's News: A Study of CBS Evening News, NBC Nightly News, Newsweek and Time.* New York: Pantheon Books.

Gitlin, Todd. 1983. *Inside Prime Time.* New York: Pantheon Books.

Greenawalt, Kent 1989. *Speech, Crime, and the Uses of Language.* New York: Oxford University Press.

Grice, Herbert. 1975. Logic and conversation, in David Davidson and George Harman eds. *The Logic of Grammar.* Encino, CA: Dickenson.

Gutmann, Amy and Dennis Thompson. 1996. *Democracy and Disagreement.* Cambridge: Belknap Press of Harvard University Press.

Habermas, Jurgen. 1982. A reply to my critics, in John Thompson, and David Held eds. *Habermas: Critical Debates.* Cambridge: MIT Press.

  1984. *The Theory of Communicative Action: Volume 1 Reason and the Rationalization of Society.* Boston: Beacon Press.

  1996. *Between Facts and Norms: Contributions to a Discourse Theory of Law and Democracy.* Cambridge: MIT Press.

Herbst, Susan. 1993. *Numbered Voices: How Opinion Polling has Shaped American Politics.* Chicago: University of Chicago Press.

Hinich, Melvin and Michael Munger. 1994. *Ideology and the Theory of Political Choice.* Ann Arbor: University of Michigan Press.

Hirschleifer, Jack. 1989. Conflict and rent-seeking success functions: ratio vs. difference models of relative success. *Public Choice* 63:101–12.

Hotelling, Harold. 1929. Stability in competition. *Economic Journal* 39:41–57.

Hovland, Carl. 1959. Reconciling conflicting results derived from experimental and survey studies of attitude change. *American Psychologist* 14:8–17.

Iyengar, Shanto and Adam Simon. 1993. News coverage of the Gulf crisis and public opinion. *Communication Research* 34:365–83.

Iyengar, Shanto and Donald Kinder. 1987. *News that Matters.* Chicago: University of Chicago Press.

Jacobs, Larry and Robert Shapiro. 1994. Issues, candidate image, and priming. *American Political Science Review* 83:399–419.

Jacobson, Gary. 1983. *The Politics of Congressional Elections.* Boston: Little, Brown.

Jacobson, Gary and Samuel Kernell. 1981. *Strategy and Choice in Congressional Elections.* New Haven: Yale University Press.

Jamieson, Kathleen. 1984. *Packaging the Presidency: A History and Criticism of Presidential Campaign Advertising.* New York: Oxford University Press.

Jennings, M. Kent and Robert Niemi. 1981. *Generations and Politics: A Panel Study of Young Adults and Their Parents.* Princeton: Princeton University Press.

Johnson, James. 1993. Is talk really cheap? Prompting conversation between critical theory and rational choice. *American Political Science Review* 87:74–86.

Jones, Bryan. 1994. *Reconceiving Decision-Making in Democratic Politics: Attention, Choice and Public Policy.* Chicago: University of Chicago Press.

Kahneman, Daniel, Paul Slovic, and Amos Tversky. 1982. *Judgment Under Uncertainty: Heuristics and Biases.* Cambridge: Cambridge University Press.

Kelley, Stanley. 1960. *Political Campaigning: Problems in Creating an Informed Electorate.* Washington D.C.: Brookings Institution.

Kernell, Samuel. 1988. *Going Public.* Washington D.C.: Congressional Quarterly Press.

Key, V. O. 1966. *The Responsible Electorate.* Cambridge: Harvard University Press.

Kinder, Donald and Lynn Sanders. 1996. *Divided by Color: Racial Politics and Democratic Ideals.* Chicago: University of Chicago Press.

Kingwell, Mark. 1995. *A Civil Tongue: Justice, Dialogue and the Politics of Pluralism.* University Park, PA: Penn State Press.

Klapper, Joseph. 1960. *The Effects of Mass Communication.* Glencoe, IL: The Free Press.

Krosnick, John and Donald Kinder. 1990. Altering the foundations of presidential support through priming. *American Political Science Review* 84:497–512.

Lasch, Christopher. 1995. *The Revolt of the Elites: and the Betrayal of Democracy.* New York: W. W. Norton.

Lazarsfeld, Paul, Berovard Berelson, and Hazel Gaudet. 1948. *The People's Choice.* New York: Columbia University Press.

Lindblom, Charles. 1977. *Politics and Markets: The World's Political Economic Systems.* New York: Basic Books.

Lodge, Milton and Robert Hamill. 1986. A partisan schema for political information processing. *American Political Science Review* 80.

Lubenow, Gerald. 1995. *California Votes – The 1994 Governor's Race: An Inside Look at the Candidates and their Campaigns by the People who Managed Them.* Berkeley: Institute of Governmental Studies Press.

Luskin, Robert. 1987. Measuring political sophistication. *American Journal of Political Science* 31:856–99.

Manin, Bernard. 1987. On legitimacy and political deliberation. *Political Theory* 15:349.

Mansbridge, Jane. 1980. *Beyond Adversary Democracy.* New York: Basic Books.

Miller, Warren and Merrill Shanks. 1996. *The New American Voter.* Cambridge: Harvard University Press.

Mutz, Diana. 1992. Mass media and the depoliticization of personal experience. *American Journal of Political Science* 36:483–508.

Nemeth, Charlan. 1995. Dissent as driving cognition, attitudes and judgments. *Social Cognition* 13:273–91.

Nie, Norman, Sydney Verba, and John Petrocik. 1976. *The Unchanging American Voter.* Cambridge: Harvard University Press.

Niemi, Robert and Herbert Weisberg. 1993. *Classics in Voting Behavior.* Washington D.C.: Congressional Quarterly Press.

O'Neill, Shane. 1997. *Impartiality in Context: Grounding Justice in a Pluralist World.* Albany, NY: SUNY Press.

Page, Benjamin and Robert Shapiro. 1992. *The Rational Public: Fifty Years of Trends in Americans' Policy Preferences.* Chicago: University of Chicago Press.

Page, Benjamin. 1996. *Who Deliberates? Mass Media in Modern Democracy.* Chicago: University of Chicago Press.

Palfrey, Thomas and Howard Rosenthal. 1985. Vote participation and strategic uncertainty. *American Political Science Review* 79:62–78.

Patterson, Thomas. 1993. *Out of Order.* New York: Alfred A. Knopf.

Petrocik, John. 1996. Issue ownership in presidential elections. *American Journal of Political Science* 54:825–50.

Petty, Richard and Paul Cacioppo. 1986. *Communication and Persuasion: Central and Peripheral Routes to Attitude Change.* New York: Springer-Verlag.

Plott, Charles. 1967. A notion of equilibrium and its possibility under majority rule. *American Economic Review* 68:146–60.

Polsby, Nelson. 1983. *Consequences of Party Reform.* Oxford: Oxford University Press.

Polsby, Nelson and Aaron Wildavsky. 1991. *Presidential Elections: Contemporary Strategies of American Electoral Politics.* New York: The Free Press.

Popkin, Samuel. 1991. *The Reasoning Voter.* Chicago: University of Chicago.

Rainey, Randall R. and William Rehg. 1996. The marketplace of ideas, the public interest, and federal regulation of the electronic media: implications of Habermas' theory of democracy. *Southern California Law Review* 69:1923–87.

Rawls, John. 1971. *A Theory of Justice.* Cambridge: Belknap Press of Harvard University Press.

1993. *Political Liberalism.* New York: Columbia University Press.

1997. The idea of public reason revisited. *University of Chicago Law Review* 64:123–59.

Reiss, Hans. 1970. *Kant's Political Writings.* Cambridge: Cambridge University Press.

Repass, David. 1971. Issue salience and party choice. *American Political Science Review* 6:389–400.

Riker, William. 1986. *The Art of Political Manipulation.* New Haven: Yale University Press.

1996. *The Strategy of Rhetoric: Campaigning for the American Constitution.* New Haven: Yale University Press.

Robson, John. 1977. *Collected Writings of John Stuart Mill*, vol. 19. Toronto: University of Toronto Press.

Salmore, Steven and Betsy Salmore. 1985. *Candidates, Parties and Campaigns.* Washington D.C.: CQ Press.

Scanlon, Thomas. 1982. Contractualism and utilitarianism, in Amartya Sen, and Bernard Williams eds. *Utilitarianism and Beyond.* Cambridge: Cambridge University Press.

Shepsle, Kenneth. 1972. The strategy of ambiguity. *American Political Science Review* 66:555–69.

Sigal, Leon. 1973. *Reporters and Officials.* Lexington, MA: D.C. Heath.

Smith, Eric. 1989. *The Unchanging American Voter.* Berkeley: University of California Press.

Sniderman, Paul, Richard Brody, and Phillip Tetlock. 1993. *Reasoning and Choice: Explorations in Political Psychology.* New York: Cambridge University Press.

Sourauf, Frank. 1992. *Inside Campaign Finance: Myths and Realities.* New Haven: Yale University Press.

Stokes, Donald. 1966. Some dynamic elements in contests for the presidency. *American Political Science Review* 60:19–28.

Sullivan, John, James Piereson, and George Marcus. 1978. Ideological constraint in the mass public: a methodological critique and some new findings. *American Journal of Political Science* 22:233–49.

Sundquist, James. 1973. *Dynamics of the Party System; Alignment and Realignment of Political Parties in the United States.* Washington D.C.: The Brookings Institution.

Tuchman, Gay. 1978. *Making News: A Study in the Construction of Reality.* New York: The Free Press.

Walzer, Michael. 1994. *Thick and Thin: Moral Argument and Home and Abroad.* Notre Dame: University of Notre Dame Press.

    1989–90. A critique of philosophical conversation. *Philosophical Forum* 21:182–96.

    1983. *Spheres of Justice: A Defense of Pluralism and Equality.* Oxford: Basil Blackwell Press.

Wattenberg, Martin. 1986. *The Decline of American Political Parties, 1952–1984.* Cambridge: Harvard University Press.

Westlye, Mark. 1991. *Senate Elections and Campaign Intensity.* Baltimore: The Johns Hopkins Press.

Wittman, Donald. 1983. Candidate motivation: a synthesis of alternative theories. *American Political Science Review* 72:18–90.

    1990. Spatial strategies when candidates have policy preferences, in James Enelow, and Melvin Hinich eds. *Advances In the Spatial Theory of Voting.* New York: Cambridge University Press.

Wright, Gerald and Mark Berkman. 1986. Candidates and policy in United States Senate elections. *American Political Science Review* 80:567–88.

Young, Iris. 1990. *Justice and the Politics of Difference.* Princeton: Princeton University Press.

Zaller, John. 1992. *The Nature and Origins of Mass Opinion.* New York: Cambridge University Press.

Index

DATE DUE

GAYLORD			PRINTED IN U.S.A.